Grant Hill

By John Rolfe and Dalton Ross

A *Sports Illustrated For Kids* Book

Grant Hill by John Rolfe and Dalton Ross

SPORTS ILLUSTRATED FOR KIDS and **KiDS** are registered trademarks of Time Inc.

Cover and insert design by Emily Peterson Perez
Cover photograph by Fernando Medina/NBA Photos
Interior design by Miriam Dustin

Grant Hill is published by SPORTS ILLUSTRATED FOR KIDS, a division of Time Inc. Its trademark is registered in the U.S. Patent and Trademark Office and in other countries. SPORTS ILLUSTRATED FOR KIDS, 135 West 50th Street, New York, NY 10020

For information, address: SPORTS ILLUSTRATED FOR KIDS

ISBN 1-930623-21-6

Printed in the United States of America

10 9 8 7 6 5 4 3 2 1

Grant Hill is a production of SPORTS ILLUSTRATED FOR KIDS Books:
Cathrine Wolf, Assistant Managing Editor; Emily Peterson Perez,
Art Director; Margaret Sieck, John Rolfe (project editor) Senior Editors;
Aaron Derr, Associate Editor; Kathleen Fieffe, Reporter; Robert J. Rohr,
Copy Editor; Ron Beuzenburg, Production Manager

CONTENTS

This book is dedicated to my wife, best friend,
and "biggest fan" — Victoria Anne Rolfe —
who breathlessly hangs on every word I write.
— John Rolfe

To Christina Kelly and Mr. Havarti Whiskers,
for their support, love, and inspiration
in everything I do.
— Dalton Ross

New Magic

When the staff of the RDV Sportsplex, in Orlando, Florida, arrived for work early in the morning of Wednesday, September 13, 2000, they saw something amazing. There was superstar Grant Hill, running, shooting, doing agility drills, lifting weights — basically doing anything he could to improve his game.

Why was it amazing? Grant had been the last person to leave the night before. He had shot baskets until 9 P.M. Grant had broken his left ankle a few months earlier. Doctors had inserted a plate, held by five screws, into his ankle. Doctors told him it would be nine months before he would be 100 percent. But Grant refused to let it take that long. He wanted to show his new teammates on the Orlando Magic that no one works harder than Grant Hill.

Basketball fans in Detroit, Michigan, long knew that about Grant. For six seasons with the Detroit Pistons, he had put his heart and soul into being the team's best player. Now Grant was starting afresh with the Magic.

Grant joined the Magic on August 3, 2000. He was a free agent and a number of teams tried to get Grant to sign with them. He picked Orlando because he was impressed by Magic head coach Glen "Doc" Rivers. He liked the way Doc got his players to give their best efforts. Even when they didn't have the most talent on the court, the Magic always seemed to give 100 percent. Grant wanted to be a part of that spirit.

"I've been a big fan of this organization from afar,"Grant said. "It's truly a blessing to be able to play where you want to play."

Grant wasn't the only one excited about his move to Orlando. Tracy McGrady, a star guard/forward for the Toronto Raptors, decided to join the Magic, in large part because he wanted to play with Grant. The Magic's senior vice president, Julius "Dr. J" Erving, called signing Grant and Tracy "the most significant day in the history of the franchise."

With Grant on board, Orlando's players and fans were beginning to dream championship dreams.

Big expectations have followed Grant during much of his life. His father, Calvin Hill, is a former All-Pro NFL running back. Grant and his family lived in the limelight that came from his dad's fame. When Grant flashed a lot of basketball talent as a kid, the attention on him increased. In high school, Grant was the best player on his basketball team. In college, at Duke University, he helped the Blue Devils reach the NCAA Championship game three times and win it twice.

"Grant Hill is the best player I've ever coached," said Mike Krzyzewski *[shah-SHEF-ski]*, the Blue Devil head coach.

Grant was chosen third by the Detroit Pistons in the 1994 NBA draft. He quickly became a sensation. He was named the 1994–95 NBA co-Rookie of the Year, along with Jason Kidd of the Dallas Mavericks. In his second season, Grant led the NBA in triple-doubles (10 or more points, rebounds, and assists in a game (see box). In his third season, Grant was named to the All-NBA First Team and won the IBM Award for all-around contributions to his team's success. That season, he was the only player in the NBA to lead his team in scoring (21.4 points per game), rebounds (9.0) and assists (7.3). Grant also was a member of Dream Team III, the U.S. basketball squad that won the Olympic gold medal in 1996.

"Grant is the ultimate impact player, the complete package," says former Piston teammate Joe Dumars. Joe played with Grant during his first five seasons, and helped him grow into the superstar he is today.

Grant is very versatile. He can shoot, dunk, pass, rebound, and play tough defense. He can play forward and guard positions. But what makes him a truly special player is his mind. Grant is smart.

"He really understands the game," says former Piston head coach Don Chaney. Coach Chaney worked with Grant during his rookie season in the NBA. "That's common among the great players like [former Boston Celtic] Larry Bird or [former Los Angeles Laker] Magic Johnson. It's something that you can't teach."

Although his talent is huge, it is Grant's humble nature that has made him one of the NBA's most popular players. His parents had money, and he lived in a big house when he was growing up, but Grant didn't want people to think he was better than they were. He was also afraid that people would like him only because of his famous dad.

As a 6' 3" freshman in high school, Grant had to be talked into playing on the varsity squad by his coach and father! Grant was worried about leaving his friends behind on the junior varsity, and he simply didn't want to stand out too much.

In college, Grant tried to stay in the shadow of his star teammates, Christian Laettner and Bobby Hurley. But it was impossible to hide how good Grant played.

In January 1995, Grant became the first rookie ever to receive the most votes from fans in the yearly selection of players for the NBA All-Star Game.

He has been named a starter by the fans every year since. But he is still surprised.

"I'm shocked at how much people like me," Grant said. "It's overwhelming."

Grant shouldn't be shocked. Many fans have grown tired of spoiled athletes who don't listen to their coaches, abuse referees, or treat fans rudely. Grant isn't that way at all. He's so polite he addresses his coaches as sir!

Off the court, Grant is bright and funny. He smiles and laughs easily. He loves video games, surfing the net, and reading. His hobby is music. He plays the

TRIPLE-DOUBLES

A triple-double is one of the hardest things to do in basketball. It means a player reaches double digits (10 or more) in three different categories in the same game. Usually that means 10 or more points, 10 or more rebounds, and 10 or more assists. It can, however, also include blocked shots and steals.

The NBA started keeping track of triple-doubles at the start of the 1979-80 season. In his first six seasons, Grant Hill had 29 triple-doubles, moving him ahead of Michael Jordan for third place all-time.

Even harder than the triple-double is the quadruple-double. That means reaching double digits in four different categories in a single game. Only four players have ever done that!

piano and is part owner of eight popular-music radio stations.

Unlike many athletes, Grant doesn't mind being a role model. He thinks it's better for kids to look up to their parents or teachers, but says, "As long as I am a role model to whomever, I'm going to be the best one that I can and help anybody out there I can."

Even though he is a famous athlete, Grant tries to treat everyone with respect. "Just because you're the best player or you're getting more attention, it doesn't mean you're a better person," he says. "It doesn't give you special privileges."

Grant has always been one to shy away from special privileges. He knows that if you really want something, you have to work hard for it. Grant never wants to settle for good when he can can be great. And that's exactly what he showed everyone early that September morning at the RDV Sportsplex in Orlando.

The Magic opened the 2000-01 season at home on October 31 against the Washington Wizards. Grant's ankle was still sore, and he couldn't play all-out. He attempted only six shots (he sank three), but still made the most of his limited ability by dishing out 10 assists as the Magic won easily, 97–86.

The first two months of the season did not go as well. Grant's ankle proved to be a thorny problem. He was able to play in only four of Orlando's first

22 games. He still averaged a respectable 13.8 points, 6.3 rebounds, and 6.3 assists per game. Of course, Grant wanted to play, and do, a lot more.

"It's frustrating to say the least," he said, but his teammates were confident that he would overcome his injury and Orlando would soon be making Magic on the court every night.

Point guard Darrell Armstrong said, "Once he gets his full confidence back in his ankle, he's going to be all right."

Growing into the Game

Grant Henry Hill was born in the early morning of October 5, 1972, in Dallas, Texas. He is the only child of Calvin and Janet Hill. They lived in Dallas because Calvin was a star running back for the Dallas Cowboys.

Grant was a big baby. "He weighed nine pounds, six ounces, and he had a long body," Mr. Hill says. "He was the biggest baby in the nursery."

The Hills had a hard time choosing a name for their son. A couple of days after the baby was born, Mr. Hill brought his friend and teammate, Dallas Cowboy quarterback Roger Staubach, to the hospital to visit Janet and the baby.

"Janet and Roger both looked at me like, 'When are we going to name him?'" Mr. Hill recalls. "Roger said, 'You've got to get your father's name in there somewhere.' Roger knew my father well and really liked him."

Mr. Hill decided that "Grant Henry" was a good name. "Grant" was Mr. Hill's mother's last name before she married. Mr. Hill's father was named Henry.

"Grant is a great name!" said Janet and Roger. So Grant it was.

The Hills lived in Dallas until Grant was almost 2 years old. Grant was a happy and energetic child. "His grandmother says she always knew he'd be an athlete because he always had some sort of ball in his hand," Mr. Hill says.

Usually, the ball was a football. "I've been told it was the first word I ever said," Grant says. "I had a little football and helmet that I carried everywhere I went."

In 1975, Mr. Hill left the Cowboys and joined the Honolulu Hawaiians of the World Football League (WFL), which had started the year before. The family lived on the Hawaiian Island of Oahu. Mrs. Hill taught math at a local college. The family spent time together going to the beach or visiting volcanoes, such as Mauna Loa and Kilauea *[kill-ah-WAY-uh]* on the island of Hawaii.

Although Grant was very young at the time, the volcanoes made quite an impression on him. When asked about his earliest childhood memory, Grant replies, "I remember the steam from the volcanoes."

"He was frightened by it," his dad says. "Kilauea is very stark, almost like the moon."

After the WFL went out of business in 1975, Mr. Hill returned to the NFL the next season and joined the Washington Redskins. The Hills settled in Reston, Virginia. Reston is a suburban town of about 48,500 people. It is about 16 miles east of Washington, D.C.

Mr. Hill thought Reston was an ideal place to raise Grant. It was safe, and the population was very diverse. "I wanted Grant to be exposed to people who were different than him in the way they looked, or dressed, or talked," Mr. Hill says. "The idea is to learn that people can live together."

Grant was taught to respect others. He learned an important lesson one day when he was with his dad in an elevator. Grant had been watching Asian martial arts movies and a group of Asian-American kids was on the elevator. When the kids got off, Grant said, "Dad, they could have wiped you out!"

"What are you talking about?" Mr. Hill asked.

"They know kung fu," Grant replied

Mr. Hill pointed out that just because a person is Asian-American, it doesn't mean he or she automatically knows martial arts, like kung fu.

"We talked about the whole idea of stereotypes [the belief that all people of the same race or culture are alike]," Mr. Hill says. "I picked one of his friends who was black and big, and I said, 'He's not an athlete.' Grant understood that stereotypes are ridiculous."

Grant's family was a close, happy one. They were also very well off. They owned expensive cars made by Mercedes and Porsche, and lived in a big house filled with African paintings and sculpture. Grant's playroom was the basement.

"I had every toy you could think of there — trucks, cars, racetracks, everything," he says. "My friends and I would get in the basement and we would play demolition [crashing the cars and trucks together]. My mom didn't like that too much."

Grant once broke all his toys. His mom got them all repaired and then gave them back as his Christmas present!

Grant also liked music. "When he was in third grade, he heard someone play the theme from *Star Wars* on a bass guitar, so he had to have a bass," says Mr. Hill. "We got him a bass and he took lessons on the bass."

Grant started taking piano lessons when he was 9, but he quit by the time he reached high school. "It wasn't cool to take lessons," he laughs. "I had to be cool. But I wish I had stuck with it."

Sports entered the picture when Grant was about 4. He liked to throw or kick a football around with his dad in the backyard. He learned how to do the three-point stance running backs go into before the ball is snapped.

He even got to demonstrate it to other kids at the football camps his dad visited.

Mr. Hill often took Grant with him to Redskins practices and games. Grant visited the locker room and met the players. Quarterback Joe Theismann and defensive lineman Dave Butz lived near the Hills and often dropped by their house.

During the years that Mr. Hill played in the NFL, many stars were guests in Grant's home. They talked to him about life as a pro athlete and Grant learned some valuable lessons that he still keeps in mind today.

"Grant picked up a lot of things like the do's and don'ts of being in public," Mr. Hill says. "He got a sense that you have to do something with fame and fortune and that there was power in being an athlete."

TIME CAPSULE

In 1982, the year Grant turned 10 years old:

* The Los Angeles Lakers, led by rookie Magic Johnson, defeated Julius Erving and the Philadelphia 76ers four games to two to win the NBA Finals.

* The national newspaper USA Today published its first issue.

* The first official space shuttle mission was launched. The shuttle Columbia carried two satellites into orbit.

* "Thriller" by Michael Jackson became the biggest-selling record album of all-time. It has sold more than 49 million copies.

In spite of that, Grant thought of his father as just Dad. "I didn't think of him as being a superstar athlete," Grant says. "People would come up to me and say, 'Your dad is a great player.' I thought they were just saying it to be nice."

Of course, kids naturally imitate their parents. After tough games, Mr. Hill often had to put ice packs and ace bandages on his body to soothe his sore joints and bruises. Grant wrapped empty ice bags around his own knees and elbows after playing football with kids in the neighborhood.

Mr. and Mrs. Hill were loving, supportive parents, but they were also very strict. Grant's friends called his mom "The General" because she was always ordering him to follow the many rules she and Mr. Hill had made. He could only watch one or two TV shows a day. He wasn't allowed to have parties or leave his neighborhood by himself until he was 16. He could use the phone for one hour, but only on weekends.

"They were too strict, if you ask me," Grant says.

Mr. Hill disagrees with that. "I don't think that was being strict so much as demanding a certain amount of discipline," he says. "I found that discipline was very helpful to me in college and in life."

One of the rules the Hills had was that it was okay to have activities outside of school, but schoolwork always came first. Although Grant was an excellent student, he knew that if his grades started to slip, his time to play sports would be cut way back.

Grant was never pushed into sports. His parents wanted him to find his own interests. "We let him know whatever he wanted to do was fine with us," says Mr. Hill.

Well, almost anything was fine. Grant wanted to play organized football, but his dad insisted that he wait until he was in ninth grade. Mr. Hill was afraid that Grant would get hurt or be discouraged if he ended up playing for a tough, demanding coach who screamed at him a lot.

"It's funny," Grant says. "But when I was finally allowed to play football, I didn't feel like playing it anymore."

By then, Grant had gotten into soccer. He started playing in a local league when he was 5. By the time he was 9, he was good enough to make a "select" (all-star) team called the Reston 72s. (The number 72 refers to the year the kids on the team were born.)

The Reston 72s were very good. They won a state championship and traveled up and down the East Coast playing in tournaments.

"Soccer was really my first love until I got to high school," Grant says. He believes that playing the sport helped him improve his agility and gave him a quick first step. Those things are important in basketball.

Grant's love of hoops grew slowly but surely. He started playing age-group basketball when he was 7, but it wasn't much fun at first.

"I was always bigger than everybody my age," he says. "But I used to get frustrated because they would put me by the post and tell me to block shots. I never got the ball."

Mr. Hill suggested that whenever Grant grabbed a rebound, he should dribble the ball up the court himself. Grant followed his dad's advice and became a good ballhandler. He was so good by the time he was 11 that he was chosen by a local select team that played other all-star teams in the Northern Virginia area.

Grant attended summer basketball camps, but practicing was often a problem when he was home. His grandfather bought him a hoop and backboard, but there was no place to put it. The family's driveway sloped down and the backyard was all grass. The neighbors who lived two houses away had a hoop, but Grant could use it only when their kids were home. There were courts in the local playground, but Grant wasn't allowed to go there whenever he wanted.

Grant solved his practice problem by shooting a ball into a garbage can he placed against the garage door. "He spent a lot of time just dribbling and shooting," Mr. Hill says. "He would always have me out trying to take the ball away from him. I wonder if that's part of the reason that he handles the ball so well."

Grant thinks so. "I think that's one of the reasons I can dribble and pass," he says. "Because I wasn't just shooting the ball all the time."

The basketball bug really bit Grant hard around the time he was 10. His family had season tickets to Georgetown University games. Grant became a big fan of two of the Hoyas' (as Georgetown's team is called) stars: Reggie Williams and Michael Jackson. Michael had been a standout at nearby South Lakes High School, which Grant would attend.

It was around that time that Grant started getting into watching and studying videotapes of games. It was something he had seen his dad do as a pro football player. Mr. Hill often brought home tapes of football games to study opposing teams and their defenses. He frequently stopped the tape, rewound it a bit, and watched a particular play again.

Grant did the same thing with tapes of Georgetown and NBA games he made. "I used to just sit and watch tapes over and over again," he says. "Every time I watched each play, I would pick up something new."

Perhaps the most important thing Grant learned was how to think ahead on the court. He found out that if a player cuts one way or makes a particular pass or move, the defense has to react a certain way. That reaction often leaves a teammate open for a pass or shot.

"He watched things almost like he was a coach,"

Mr. Hill says. "We went to a Georgetown–Villanova game at the Final Four in Lexington, Kentucky [in 1985]. It was a close game and I was panicking. He was really into the game intellectually. He was telling me, 'This is what's happening . . .'"

After watching a tape, Grant would go outside and practice what he had just seen. He improved a lot, but he didn't realize it.

Grant liked to go to Twin Lakes Park and watch other kids play pickup games. One of the kids was Dennis Scott, who now plays for the Dallas Mavericks. Grant would be invited to play, but it took a lot to convince him to do it. "I always just thought everyone was so much better than me," he says. "But I guess that made me work harder when I played against them."

Grant wasn't the only one who didn't know how good he was. Mr. Hill didn't know how good Grant was, either. He found out when he and Grant went to St. Louis for a youth basketball tournament. Grant was 13 at the time.

One of the teams Grant played against was a squad from Detroit led by Chris Webber and Jalen Rose. Chris and Jalen later starred at Michigan and in the NBA.

"I remember looking at those kids before that game and trying to figure out how I was going to scrape Grant off the floor and pick up his spirits afterward," says Mr. Hill. "And then Grant's team won easily. I had no idea how good Grant was. That was my first glimpse."

Grant won all-tournament honors and gave his dad another glimpse of his talent once they got home.

"You think you're pretty good, huh?" said Mr. Hill. "You think you can beat your old man?"

Grant accepted the challenge and they went to the playground for a game of one-on-one. The first person to score 30 points wins.

Grant won easily.

"I kidded myself saying I'd let him get to 20 points and then stage a furious comeback," Mr. Hill says. "After I lost, we played again. I tried real hard, but it was the same thing. I wanted to throw him against the fence."

"I always knew I could beat him," Grant laughs. "He was just another chump on the court to me."

Grant's best friend, Michael Ellison, already knew how good Grant had become. They had played a lot of one-on-one together and Grant usually won.

Michael was a year older than Grant. He played on the freshman team at South Lakes High School with two of Grant's other pals, Michael Taylor and Darryl Branch. As an eighth-grader at Langston Hughes Junior High, Grant worked as waterboy for their team.

Grant was about to enter ninth grade at South Lakes and he had his heart set on playing with his friends on the junior varsity team. It was not to be.

Independence Day

Grant didn't know it, but someone important had been watching him. That someone was Wendell Byrd, the basketball coach at South Lakes High School.

Coach Byrd had been watching Grant over the years. He had seen him play in local leagues, at basketball camps, and at the tournament in St. Louis. He was very impressed by Grant's talent, knowledge of basketball, and willingness to practice.

The varsity team at South Lakes needed a player who could grab offensive rebounds and stick the ball back in the basket. Grant was 6' 3" and a good rebounder. He was exactly the kind of player the team needed.

Coach Byrd also knew that Grant was looking forward to playing on the junior varsity team with his friends. He had a strong suspicion that Grant wouldn't be crazy about the idea of playing for the varsity.

"He was the type of person who didn't want to stand out," Coach Byrd says. "He wanted everything to be smooth and nice and easy for everybody. He didn't want to make waves with his buddies. I think he felt that it may not be right for him to push ahead of them."

The day before tryouts began, Coach Byrd called Mr. Hill and told him that he wanted Grant to try out for the varsity team. Mr. Hill was excited, but worried that Grant might not get to play very much because he was only a freshman. In fact, a freshman had never started on the school's varsity team. Grant's development as a player could be delayed if he spent a lot of time on the bench.

"Grant's going to play," Coach Byrd said. "He has the ability to start."

Coach Byrd asked Mr. Hill to speak to Grant and see if he could convince him to at least give the tryout a shot.

After school the next day, all the players gathered in the school gym for tryouts. There were three courts: one each for the freshman team, the junior varsity, and the varsity. Each player was assigned to a court.

"Come on, Grant," Coach Byrd called out. "You come over here with the varsity."

Grant was shocked. His dad hadn't said anything to him yet. He worked out with the varsity players that evening, but told Coach Byrd after practice that he wasn't sure he wanted to play for the team.

"Are you better than those guys?" Coach Byrd asked, pointing at the junior varsity players.

"Yes," Grant said meekly.

"Just think about it," Coach Byrd said. "Why don't you go talk to your father?"

When Grant got home, he sat down with his father to talk over the team situation. When Mr. Hill said he thought Grant should go ahead and try out for the varsity, Grant exploded.

"I don't want to do that!" he shouted. "I want to play with my friends on the jayvee team!"

The more Mr. Hill tried to explain why he thought Grant should try out for the varsity, the more upset Grant became. Pretty soon he was in tears.

Grant accused his dad of asking Coach Byrd for the tryout. Grant had always been afraid that people would think he got special treatment because he had a famous father. One time when Grant was in eighth grade, his dad was invited to speak at his junior high school. Grant was so embarrassed that he pretended he was sick and hid in the nurse's office!

"I didn't want anybody, especially my friends, thinking I was better than them," Grant says. "My father was in sports and my parents had money. I thought if I do well in sports, people will get jealous and not like me."

Mr. Hill insisted that he had *not* asked Coach Byrd for anything. "You've got to at least try out," he told

Grant. "If it doesn't work out, it doesn't work out and you can play on the jayvee."

Grant reluctantly agreed. "Okay, I'll try out," he said. "But only because you want me to. This is like child abuse!"

Mr. Hill was stunned by Grant's remark. "I'll never forget that," he says. "I told Grant, 'You don't know what child abuse is!'"

Grant practiced with the varsity for the next four days. He did well and made the team. Best of all, his friends were excited for him. "Wow, man!" they told him. "Go for it!"

Grant was relieved. They didn't resent him after all. And when he saw that the older players on the team accepted him, he began to feel comfortable. After the first few games, he told Coach Byrd, "You were right. Things are working out. I appreciate how you felt about me."

As the season went along, Grant showed that he could do more than just rebound. He was a good shooter and passer. He averaged 9.7 points per game, but was determined to do better.

"He was the type of athlete who didn't want to just sit back," Coach Byrd says. "He wanted to improve his game."

That summer, Grant watched a lot of videotape and worked out often. He traveled to a national 14-and-under tournament in Seattle, Washington and was named the Most Valuable Player. When school began in the fall, Michael Ellison told Coach Byrd, "You should see Grant now. He's awesome!"

Grant was very happy. Michael and his other pals were now on the varsity, too. With Grant at forward and Michael at guard, the South Lakes Seahawks went on to a 21–3 record. Grant averaged 22 points and 10 rebounds per game and was named the Northern Virginia Player of the Year.

By then, Grant was getting a lot of attention. Kids at school stopped him in the hallway and asked for his autograph. Local newspapers sent reporters to cover him and write stories about him. Naturally, Grant was embarrassed. He even told his dad to stop being interviewed so much so that parents of other kids on the team could get in the newspaper.

Grant wasn't impressed with himself at all. He was sure that the best player on the team was Jerome Scott,

ON GUARDS

There are two guard positions on a basketball team: point guard and shooting guard. The point guard directs the team's offensive plays and must be a good ballhandler and passer. Grant developed these skills by studying videotapes of games and by practicing dribbling outside his house. The shooting guard is often a team's best shooter.

a senior guard who had been offered scholarships to Georgetown, the University of Miami, and several other schools.

Grant admired Jerome so much he often pretended to *be* him while he practiced. There were times when he went home and said to his dad, "Jerome is just always so good. He can jump so high."

"You can jump as high as he can," Mr. Hill would reply. "He's no better than you."

"Oh yes he is!" Grant insisted.

Well, no, he wasn't. As a junior, Grant averaged 18 points per game and broke Jerome's all-time school career scoring record of 1,288 points. To top that off, Grant led the Seahawks to a 27–2 record and their first ever northern region championship.

Grant also expanded his game during his junior season. Coach Byrd made his players practice playing different positions and Grant worked hard at learning to play guard, instead of forward.

"Grant really took it as a challenge to master the skills he needed to play guard," Coach Byrd says. "By the time he was a senior, he was the best ballhandler on the team."

Once again, Grant was named the Northern Virginia Player of the Year. And that summer, he attended the prestigious Five-Star Summer Basketball Camp, where only the best high school players go. And of all of them, who was chosen MVP of the all-star game? Grant! His performance made the camp's director gush, "If Grant Hill is not All-America, there is no America!"

Talk about a confidence-booster! "After that, I kind of realized I was one of the better players in the area," Grant says. "Looking back, I was a lot better than I gave myself credit for."

Grant had grown to be 6' 8" tall during high school. That's tall for a guard, and some people thought Coach Byrd was nuts to play him at any position other than forward. But he was only taking advantage of Grant's height. "He could see over defenses," Coach Byrd says.

Grant capped off his high school career with a smashing senior season in 1989–90. The Seahawks were 25–4 as Grant averaged 25.5 points, 11 rebounds, and 8 assists per game. He won All-America honors and his third straight Northern Virginia Player of the Year Award.

Naturally, many colleges were interested in Grant. He had been receiving scholarship offers since his freshman year. Now he was getting about 20 letters a day from schools that wanted him to play for them. "He was the premier player that people wanted," Coach Byrd says.

College coaches were impressed by how much Grant knew about basketball. Mr. Hill remembers visiting the University of North Carolina and taking a walk while Grant met with head coach Dean Smith. "When I came back, Coach Smith told me that Grant already knew most of their plays," Mr. Hill says. "I think it was because he had watched so much tape of North Carolina and had tried to analyze it."

Choosing which college to attend was a big decision. Grant's parents had always stressed the importance of getting a good education. Mr. and Mrs. Hill attended colleges that were famous for being excellent schools. Mr. Hill had graduated from Yale University with a degree in history. Mrs. Hill studied math at Wellesley College. Grant himself was no slacker. He had done so well in high school, he was chosen the senior class valedictorian. (A valedictorian usually has the best grades in a graduating class and gets to give the farewell speech at the graduation ceremony.)

DUKE UNIVERSITY

Duke University is one of the top colleges in America. It is located in Durham, North Carolina. Grant chose Duke, which has about 6,000 students, because it offered him the chance both to play basketball and to get a good education. Through 1998, Duke had produced 33 players who went on to play in the pros. More important, almost all of Duke's basketball players since 1977 (95 percent) have earned their degrees. At most Division I colleges, the graduation rate for basketball players is just over half (a little above 50 percent).

Grant wasn't sure what he wanted to do with his life yet. He had begun to dream about playing in the NBA, but he knew how tough it is to become a pro athlete. His dad had told him that the odds of becoming a pro athlete were slim for anyone. Grant also knew that the average NBA career lasts only six years. Decisions, decisions!

Mr. Hill thought Grant should go to the University of North Carolina. Mrs. Hill thought Georgetown University was best. Both are excellent colleges. Grant chose Duke University, which is in North Carolina. He thought it offered him the best of both worlds. It has a top basketball program and is also famous for making sure that athletes get their degrees.

"I thought if I go there and do well, I'll have an opportunity to make it to the NBA," he says. "But I always questioned my ability and doubted whether or not I could make it. That's one of the reasons why I picked Duke. I thought if I didn't play pro ball, a good education would set me up for something else."

Michael Ellison says there was another reason behind Grant's decision: He wanted to make his own choice. "I definitely think it was Grant's independence day the day he picked Duke," Michael says.

Grant's years at Duke would turn out to be an exciting and productive time. Most important, he would discover the self-confidence he needed to go on to even bigger and better things.

Not Your Average Dad

Sons of famous athletes are often compared to their fathers. But in the case of Grant and his father, Calvin, it's much harder. Mr. Hill played a different sport. But if you look closely at their personalities and the way they live their lives, you'll see they have a lot in common. You will also notice some similarities in the way they were raised by their parents.

"Grant is so incredibly like Calvin," says Janet Hill. "They're both so serious."

In spite of the similarity, Grant and his dad grew up in very different situations. Grant was born into a well-to-do family. Calvin's parents weren't poor, but they couldn't offer Calvin the kinds of luxuries that Grant had as a kid, such as a big house, fancy cars, and lots of toys. But Grant and Calvin both became famous pro athletes the same way: by hard work and discipline.

Calvin Hill was born on January 2, 1947, in Baltimore, Maryland. Like Grant, he was an only child and a large baby, although not as big as Grant. Calvin weighed 8½ pounds. He also showed signs of being athletic at an early age. As a toddler, Calvin was always playing with or throwing a ball.

Calvin's parents were Henry and Elizabeth Hill. They had moved to Baltimore from North Carolina during the Great Depression of the 1930's *(see box, page 34)*. Henry Hill did not have much formal education. He worked on construction projects and took a job in Baltimore as a crew foreman in a boiler factory. The job paid him enough to buy a simple two-story house.

Surviving hard times made Calvin's dad appreciate the value of hard work. "My dad admired people who worked hard," Calvin says. "When he worked, he wanted to be the best guy in his construction crew."

Calvin's dad believed that people should always try their hardest at whatever they did. "When I went away to school, the only thing my father would say to me is there's going to be people who are smarter than you and faster than you, but nobody can outwork you," Calvin says. He learned the lesson and passed it along to Grant.

Calvin's parents also taught him to respect other people and *their* feelings. This later ended up being applied to them! When Calvin became a pro football player, he felt uncomfortable about being paid a lot more money than his dad had ever been able to earn.

"I was very conscious of his feelings," Calvin says. "I didn't want him to think my salary made me superior to him. He used to joke about it and say, 'You have more money than me. I guess I can't tell you what to do.'"

Earlier in life, Calvin's parents had always told him what to do. They were as strict with him as he later was with Grant. Calvin's neighborhood wasn't the safest place in the world and his parents were worried about Calvin hanging out with bad people in the wrong places. They insisted on knowing where he was at all times and kept him occupied with activities, such as violin lessons, outside of school.

Calvin may not have always liked living by strict rules, but he got the message his parents were trying

THE GREAT DEPRESSION

On "Black Thursday," which was October 24, 1929, the economy of the United States collapsed. Banks, stores, businesses, and factories started going out of business. Millions of people lost their jobs, their savings, and their homes. The Great Depression affected just about every country in the world. In the United States, the economy began to improve after Franklin D. Roosevelt became president in 1933. He created a series of programs called "The New Deal" that helped put people back to work. But the Great Depression didn't end until after the U.S. entered World War II in December 1941 — 12 years after Black Thursday.

to send: They loved him. "My father used to say that discipline is a form of caring," he says.

Being an only child, Calvin spent a lot of time alone. He says he still enjoys his own company. Grant is the same way. He often goes to video arcades, movies, and restaurants by himself.

As a kid, Calvin read a lot and it paid off in the class-room. His grades in junior high were so good he won a scholarship to the Riverdale School, a boarding school for boys in New York City.

"It was very strict," he says. "Every night during the week, you had only thirty minutes of free time after seven o'clock."

Calvin had always liked sports. He had played Little League baseball and recreation-league basketball. He didn't play football until he got to Riverdale, however.

Mr. Hill still hasn't forgotten his first day of practice. "I put the thigh pads on wrong," he says. "It was pretty clear that I needed a lot of training." It's hard to believe that just eight years later, he was an NFL star!

Calvin was a naturally gifted athlete, and he did some amazing things in his four years at Riverdale. He was a star pitcher who batted over .400 for the baseball team. In basketball, he averaged 26 points per game and won all-city honors. Once he learned how to play football, he quarterbacked the school team to 51 wins in a row!

Calvin graduated from Riverdale with honors and accepted an academic scholarship to Yale University, an Ivy League school, instead of a sports scholarship to another school. He didn't expect to play in the NFL, so he didn't want sports to interfere with his schoolwork. Accepting a sports scholarship would have required him to focus most of his time and attention on football.

"I liked the idea of not having to play football if I didn't want to," he says.

Calvin studied history at Yale and decided to go out for the football team anyway. He was switched to running back, and went on to win All-America honors. He also set a school record by scoring 144 points.

Calvin and quarterback Brian Dowling became such big stars at Yale that a classmate named Garry Trudeau created characters based on them in a comic strip for the campus newspaper. The strip, called "Doonesbury," is now in newspapers nationwide. Calvin's character no longer appears, but Brian's "B.D." is still a regular.

If you read old newspaper and magazine stories about Calvin during his college years, you will be surprised by how much like Grant he was. Reporters described him as friendly and thoughtful. He tutored and counseled high school kids. He admired civil rights leader Dr. Martin Luther King, Jr., and joined programs to help the African-American people.

During the fall of 1968, Calvin went to a party after the Yale-Harvard football game. It was there that he met a math student from Wellesley College named Janet McDonald. Calvin and Janet started dating. One of Janet's college roommates was Hillary Rodham. Hillary later married Bill Clinton, the future President of the United States. Two years after Calvin and Janet started dating, they married.

Calvin graduated from Yale with a degree in history in 1969. That summer, he was chosen by the Dallas Cowboys in the first round of the NFL draft. The team's scouting report on Calvin said he had "size, skill, strength, speed, and unlimited spirit. He has every physical and mental quality." As it happens, NBA scouts

IVY LEAGUERS IN THE NFL

Yale University is one of eight colleges that make up the "Ivy League." (The nickname is said to come from the ivy that grows on many of the buildings on each campus.) The others are Brown, Columbia, Cornell, Dartmouth, Harvard, the University of Pennsylvania, and Princeton.

Ivy League schools are better known for high academic standards than for producing pro athletes. But Calvin Hill is one of more than 156 Ivy Leaguers who have played in the NFL. The most famous are quarterback Sid Luckman (Columbia), who played for the Chicago Bears from 1939 to 1950, and linebacker Chuck Bednarik (Pennsylvania), who played for the Philadelphia Eagles from 1949 to 1962. Both men were elected to the Pro Football Hall of Fame.

have used much the same words to describe Grant!

Calvin made a splash in the NFL during his first season. He gained 942 yards, scored eight touchdowns, and was chosen over O.J. Simpson of the Buffalo Bills for the NFL Rookie of the Year award. Calvin probably would have led the league in rushing that year if he had not hurt his foot in the ninth game of the season.

Cowboy head coach Tom Landry was so impressed that he told reporters, "Hill might be the best ballcarrier I've seen in 20 years of football." That was great praise indeed because Coach Landry had seen many Pro Football Hall of Fame running backs over the years.

Calvin helped the Cowboys reach the Super Bowl during his second season. They lost to the Baltimore Colts, 16–13, in a heart-stopping game that was decided by a field goal in the final seconds. The next year, they made it back to the big game and made up for the defeat by flattening the Miami Dolphins, 24–3.

Calvin didn't get to play much in either Super Bowl. Duane Thomas was the team's number-one running back during those years. But in 1972, Calvin got a chance to take over. He became the first player in Cowboys history to rush for more than 1,000 yards in a season. He was also selected to play in his first Pro Bowl. The year was made even better by Grant's birth.

Calvin's best NFL season was in 1973 when he

rushed for a career-high total of 1,142 yards. In 1975, he left the Cowboys when the Honolulu Hawaiians of the World Football League (WFL) offered him much more money. (The World Football League existed from October 1973 to October 1975.) Calvin signed a three-year contract, but ended up playing in only two games before the WFL went out of business.

When Calvin returned to the NFL in 1976, it was as a backup player for the Washington Redskins. He never gained more than 301 yards in a season, but his ability to catch passes still made him a valuable player.

In August 1978, Calvin announced his retirement but he changed his mind two weeks later and joined the Cleveland Browns. Mr. Hill decided, however, not to move his family to Cleveland. Grant and his mother were able to fly to Cleveland for his dad's home games, but Mr. Hill was away from home more than ever. Grant says he only saw him six or seven times during the football season.

"I'd come home sometimes on my off day, but it was difficult," Calvin says. "I'd call Janet and we'd talk about what was happening with Grant."

With his dad away, Grant grew closer to his mother. "We got to know each other inside out," he says.

Mrs. Hill took Grant to his soccer and basketball games and became his biggest fan. "She didn't know too much about the games, but she clapped and cheered," Grant says with a laugh. "She didn't know what she was clapping and cheering about, but she was the loudest one there."

Grant's mom taught him a valuable lesson during those years: Honor your commitments. "I played different sports, so there were times I had maybe two or three games in one day," he says. "After a game, I wouldn't want to play anymore. I'd be tired. She was like, 'Hey, you committed to it, you have to go play.'"

Mrs. Hill had a lot of commitments of her own. She ran her own consulting firm in Washington, D.C. (Her firm helps corporations find better ways to do business.) She was very busy, but she always found time for her son. Each day at 4 P.M., she would call Grant to talk about her day and what was going on with him.

When his parents were at work, Grant went to the home of a local family after school. "They were foster parents," he says. "They always had kids of all different ages. I think that's when I started to enjoy being with kids and working with them."

Calvin Hill retired from pro football in 1981 after 13 seasons. He was 35 years old. He took a job with the Browns working with players who had problems with drugs. Now Mr. Hill is a consultant with the Cowboys. He helps players with off-the-field issues, such as finances and preparations for life after football. He also does his own consulting work. He is in the real-estate business with former teammate Roger Staubach. In

1998, Mr. Hill and some partners tried unsuccessfully to buy the Cleveland Browns football team.

Once Calvin's pro career ended, he was able to focus more of his attention on his son. He went to all of Grant's games. Grant appreciated having his dad around more, but sometimes it caused problems.

"It was really bad in high school," Grant told reporter Michael Geffner of *The Sporting News*. "Whatever I scored or whatever I did would never be enough for him."

Calvin admits he expects a lot of Grant, but he says he just wants him to strive for excellence every time he plays. "I'm always looking for the perfect game out of him," Mr. Hill says. "And I know it will never happen. But that's not a reason to stop trying. I've always wanted things to be perfect for him."

Grant thinks he and his father may look at sports differently because they played different sports. "My dad's got that football mentality," Grant says. "He wants me to show intensity all the time and get angry at every mistake. What he doesn't understand is as much as he wants for me, I want even more. I just don't show it on my face. I keep my emotions inside. But I'm harder on me than he ever could be.

"In a way, I'm lucky," Grant continues. "It would have been much worse if I played football. I've tried to discover my own place. That's why I play basketball. I guess I'm making my name for myself."

At Duke University, that's just what Grant would do.

The Tall Guy Down the Hall

When Grant arrived at Duke, in the fall of 1990, he was surprised by the fuss people made about him. He was shy and quiet. He just wanted to get used to college life and blend in with his teammates. "The first day, there were people asking me for my autograph and they were expecting so much," he says.

The Duke Blue Devils were a talented team led by junior center Christian Laettner [LATE-ner] and sophomore guard Bobby Hurley. The season before, Duke had had a 29–9 record and reached the Final Four of the NCAA tournament for the third year in a row. In the national championship game, the Blue Devils were crushed by the University of Nevada–Las Vegas (UNLV) Runnin' Rebels, 103–73. It was the most lopsided score in NCAA tournament finals history.

Grant was one of five freshmen on the 1990–91 Blue Devils. Head coach Mike Krzyzewski was expecting good things from his young team. He was excited about Grant's ability to play different positions.

"He has a special mind for the game," Coach K told reporters. "Grant will just play all over. There's not an aspect of the game he doesn't do well. He can play point guard, he can play inside [close to the basket], and he's a good passer."

Duke's fans saw Grant play for the first time when the Blue Devils opened their season on November 14. They played Marquette University in a game at Cameron Indoor Stadium, Duke's home arena.

The sellout crowd of 9,314 saw Grant play all five

COACH K

Mike Krzyzewski [sha-SHEF-ski] is the winningest coach in the history of Duke University. From 1980 through 1998, he had led the Blue Devils to 14 NCAA Tournament appearances, seven Final Fours, and two national championships. More important, Coach K is dedicated to making sure his players graduate. All but three of his 61 scholarship players have graduated. Two of the three who did not were on the 1990 team that reached the Final Four. Banners honoring Duke's Final Four teams hang in Cameron Indoor Stadium. But until the two players from the 1990 team return to Duke and complete their degrees, Coach K will refuse to display that team's banner.

positions and score 12 points. He got most of them by making dazzling inside moves while he was playing forward. Grant got a chance to take over for Bobby at point guard and the offense didn't miss a beat. The Blue Devils won easily, 87–74.

"I didn't expect us to be this good defensively this early in the season," Coach K told reporters after another game. "I'm excited about our defense."

G rant was off to a great start, on the court and off. Outside of basketball, he was still getting used to college life. He hadn't decided what subject he wanted to major in. (He later chose history, the same subject his dad had studied.) He also discovered the responsibilities of living on his own in a college dorm.

One day, Grant lost the key to his dorm room and was too embarrassed to ask for another one. He had to leave the door unlocked, although he pretended to lock his door each time he left. He didn't get a new key for a month! His telephone was disconnected at one point because he forgot to pay his bill. Later that season, he forgot to pick his dad up at the airport when Mr. Hill flew in for a visit.

"Yeah, he's still eighteen years old," Mr. Hill sighed to reporter Anthony Cotton of *The Washington Post.*

One of the things Grant says he enjoyed most about life in college was just being accepted by the other students in the dorm. He was known as "Grant, the Tall

Guy Down the Hall," not "Grant, the Basketball Player." He also spent time hanging out with his teammates and getting to know them. He roomed with forward Antonio Lang.

As the season rolled along, the Blue Devils continued to show that they were very good. On March 3, the Blue Devils won the Atlantic Coast Conference regular-season championship by beating their fiercest rivals, the University of North Carolina Tar Heels, 83–77. (UNC is in Chapel Hill, only 25 miles away from Durham, where Duke is located.)

The Blue Devils were feeling pretty good when they met the Tar Heels again a week later in the ACC tournament championship game. But they didn't feel good for long. They suddenly found themselves trailing the Tar Heels by 10 points. They got frustrated and started to complain about the referees' calls.

The Blue Devils went to their locker room at half-time trailing, 49–36. They should have stayed there. They played no better in the second half and ended up losing, 96–74.

It was a very embarrassing defeat. The Blue Devils had been lazy and, even worse, they had lost their cool. This could be a problem — the NCAA tournament was coming up.

After the defeat by North Carolina, Coach K wrote "0–0" on the blackboard in the locker room. He was telling his players that they would be starting out with a clean record in the upcoming NCAA tournament. They had to learn from the loss to North Carolina and play harder. "If we don't, then we're fools and we lose," the coach said.

Coach K later told Grant to play more aggressively. Grant often seemed as if he were trying not to get in the way of his teammates. "When you dunk, you're not in the way," he told Grant. "Don't be afraid to make a mistake. Don't be afraid to be good. You can be a threat on offense if you assert yourself and be more creative."

It was the most important basketball advice Grant *ever* received, but it took time to sink in fully.

The 1991 NCAA tournament began on March 14. The Blue Devils came out on fire. They zipped through the first four games. Grant averaged a solid 9.5 points, 5 rebounds, and 2.5 assists in the four games, but Bobby Hurley was the big star. His 20 points against St. John's earned him the Regional Final MVP award.

Duke's next stop was the Final Four at the Hoosier Dome, in Indianapolis, Indiana. When the Blue Devils arrived, a monster was waiting for them: the UNLV Runnin' Rebels. The Runnin' Rebs were 34–0 and were on a 45-game winning streak.

The Blue Devils wanted to get back at UNLV for the embarrassing loss in the 1990 championship game, but few people thought they had a chance. Coach K knew his team could win, but only if it played with confidence and enthusiasm.

To get his players ready for battle, Coach K made them watch a tape of the first six minutes of their championship game loss to UNLV the season before. They had been flat and were hammered right from the opening buzzer.

The Blue Devils got the picture and came out fighting this time. It was a very rough game. UNLV was an aggressive team. The Rebels were called for "charging" (running into a defensive player who is in a set position) 20 times. Midway through the second half, Anderson Hunt of UNLV was running downcourt on a breakaway when Bobby Hurley slammed him hard. A foul was called, but Bobby had delivered a message: the Blue Devils were not intimidated.

When the dust began to settle, the Blue Devils found themselves down, 76–71, with a little more than two minutes to play. Bobby sank a 3-point shot that made the score, 76–74. Then the rest of the team caught fire.

Duke's defense clamped down on UNLV and did not allow the Rebels to take a shot. Grant was quietly chipping in with his usual well-rounded game: 11 points, 5 assists, and 5 rebounds.

The biggest moment of the game came when Blue Devil Brian Davis was fouled after making a layup. He sank a free throw that put Duke ahead, 77–76. For the first time that season, mighty UNLV was in a close game with time running out.

Larry Johnson tied the score with a free throw, but Christian was fouled with only 12.7 seconds left to play. He calmly stepped to the line and sank two free throws. A desperate UNLV shot at the buzzer failed to go in and Duke had achieved an amazing 79–77 upset.

After the game, Coach K praised his team's grace under pressure. "Put yourself in their place," he told reporters. "I'm amazed they can perform like that with so much on the line."

The Blue Devils were celebrating, but Coach K forced them to get their minds back on business in a hurry. The title game — against the University of Kansas Jayhawks — was only two nights away. "An ordinary team would be satisfied beating UNLV, but an ordinary team won't win on Monday," he said.

The Blue Devils were extremely confident they would win. Even Grant was predicting victory.

In a news conference the night before the game, Grant told reporters he would be disappointed if Duke lost. Grant's confidence stunned his dad. Mr. Hill says, "I heard that and thought to myself, 'Is this the same kid who cried when he was told he was going to play on the varsity team as a freshman in high school?'"

On April 1, 1991, Duke and Kansas squared off in front of 47,100 fans in the Hoosier Dome. Grant's parents were in the stands as Grant made the most memorable play of the night.

About two minutes into the game, Bobby tossed a high "alley-oop" pass toward the basket. The ball looked as if it was going to sail out of bounds. Instead, Grant grabbed it with one hand and slammed it into the basket with a stunning jackknife dunk. Again, was this the same kid who had to be told to be aggressive? The play was shown on sports-highlight shows for weeks.

Grant's dunk seemed to set the right tone for the Blue Devils. They looked good throughout while the Jayhawks missed shots they should have made. Finally, after nine trips to the Final Four without winning a title, Duke came out on top, 72–65. Christian Laettner, although tired out, was able to score 18 points. He set a record by making all 12 of his free throws, and was named Most Valuable Player. Grant's

GRANT'S 1990-91 SEASON

* Became the first Duke freshman since Johnny Dawkins in 1982–83 to score 10 or more points in each of his first six games.

* Got Duke off to a roaring start with a stunning dunk against Kansas in the opening moments of the NCAA championship game.

* Won freshman All-America honors.

* Played on the U.S. national team at the 1991 Pan American Games and won a bronze medal.

performance was a solid 10 points and 8 rebounds.

When the final buzzer sounded, Mr. Hill noticed an expression on Grant's face. It reminded Mr. Hill of the times he used to tickle Grant when Grant was a baby. Mr. Hill was pretty tickled, too. Mrs. Hill later told *Sports Illustrated*, "I was there when he made the Pro Bowl. I was there when he won the Super Bowl. Nothing made him happier."

Grant was happy, too. "From Day One, it seemed we were destined to win it all," Grant said. "There was a special quality, a closeness, a chemistry I'd never seen on a basketball team before."

Looking back at his first year of college, Grant could see that he had changed. "Last year at this time I was very quiet and kept to myself," he said. "This year forced me to open up."

Grant's final stats (11.2 points per game, 5.1 rebounds, 2.2 assists, 51 steals) were good enough to earn him Freshman All-America honors. But he wasn't satisfied.

"I wish I could have it all back because I know I could have done more," he said. "I'm anxious for next year to start so that I can play like I know I can play right from the start."

Right from the start, Grant and the Blue Devils were gunning for another trip to the championship final. Could they do it?

Doing It All

Grant's reputation as a top college player was growing steadily. His mindbending dunk in the 1991 NCAA championship game against Kansas brought him lots of attention.

"That's the play, I guess, that sticks out from the game," Grant told reporters. "Every time someone sees me, they mention that."

One day during Grant's second season at Duke, Mr. Hill discovered just how famous his son was becoming. Mr. Hill was in a supermarket when he noticed a group of boys whispering and pointing at him. When they followed him to the checkout line, Mr. Hill thought they were going to ask him for his autograph.

"Are you Grant Hill's father?" one boy asked.

Mr. Hill was no longer "Calvin Hill, former NFL star." He was now "Grant Hill's father."

"That's the first time it happened to me," Mr. Hill told a reporter from *USA Today*. "But the problem is, I'm still getting used to reading about him."

In Grant's sophomore season, Mr. Hill would have plenty to read about. The Blue Devils began the 1991–92 season hoping to become the first team in 19 years to win two national championships in a row. They had a good chance. Four starters were back (Grant, Christian, Bobby, and Thomas Hill, who is not related to Grant). But Duke faced a tough schedule against powerful teams such as the University of Michigan and Louisiana State University (LSU). LSU was led by a 7' 1" sophomore center named Shaquille O'Neal.

Coach K was worried that the pressure of trying to win another title would distract his players, so he kept telling them, "Let's have fun."

The Blue Devils got off to a roaring start and won their first 17 games. Five of the victories were blowouts, with Duke winning by 28 points or more.

The Blue Devils felt very confident, even cocky. "We want people to fear us," forward Brian Davis told reporters.

In Duke's first 17 wins of the 1991-92 season, Grant played superbly. He scored 10 points or more in each game. On January 6, he had his best college game ever, scoring 26 points against Florida State. The Blue Devils did not lose a game until February 5, when they were upset, 75–73, by their in-state rivals, the University of North Carolina Tar Heels. The worst thing about the loss was that Bobby cracked a bone in his right foot during the game. The next day, the team doctor announced that Bobby would be out of action for about a month.

Grant was shocked when he heard the news. "I was in class and one of my friends came up and said 'Bobby's in a cast,'" Grant told reporters. "I thought he was joking."

Mr. Hill, who was visiting, knew Bobby had to be feeling bad, so he and Grant took him out to dinner. "We were just trying to get him in a good mood," Grant says. "My dad talked about what Bobby's injury was and how he'd be okay. I think that little meeting was good for Bobby and good for me."

Grant was going to take over for Bobby at point guard. Grant had the ability to do it, but there would be a lot of pressure on him. Filling Bobby's shoes was a tall order. Grant would now be the one his teammates counted on when the outcome of a game was in doubt.

"I don't like being in that situation," Grant told reporters. "I don't think of myself as a clutch player."

Grant knew he had to crank up his intensity a notch. "At times this year, I just sit back and watch," he said. "I grew up looking to keep everyone happy, and I've tried to be an unselfish player."

Grant's first test was against Shaquille O'Neal and LSU on February 8. A crowd of 13,846 fans packed the

Pete Maravich Assembly Center, in Baton Rouge, Louisiana. The game was broadcast on national TV.

Grant was nervous as he entered the arena. The excitement had grown to an intense level. "It felt like it was the Final Four or something," Coach K says.

Shaq was a monster around the basket that day. He blocked everything in sight, and even batted a shot by Brian Davis into the seats!

The Blue Devils decided there was no way to go around or through Shaq, so they fired long jump shots over him. Grant tossed in 16 points worth. During the season, he had been scoring most of his points by driving to the basket. Now he was pulling up and sinking jumpers with ease. Duke ended up winning, 77–67.

Besides his 16 points, Grant also had six assists. He had some trouble running the team's fast-break plays. The Blue Devils scored only six times on 13 fast breaks and lost possession of the ball five times. But all in all, Grant had done well.

"Grant had poise throughout the game," Coach K said.

Coach K noticed the difference between Bobby and Grant. Bobby played by instinct. Grant analyzed everything before deciding what to do. The reason, of course, was all that videotape he had studied.

Duke was 4–1 with Grant starting at point guard. He averaged 16.4 points, 6.2 rebounds, and 5.6 assists during the five games. The Blue Devils' only loss during that time was to Wake Forest on February 23.

Two days after the game, Grant twisted his right ankle in practice. It hurt a lot, and the team doctor announced that Grant could be out for four weeks. Luckily, Bobby was ready to return, and forward Antonio Lang filled in ably for Grant, who ended up missing three games. The Blue Devils won all three.

Grant returned for the final regular-season game on March 8 against the Tar Heels. The Blue Devils won, 89–77, and finished the regular season with a sparkling 25–2 record.

On March 19, the 1992 NCAA tournament began. The Blue Devils started their quest for a second straight national title by rolling over Campbell University (from North Carolina), the University of Iowa, and Seton Hall (from New Jersey). Then they ran into trouble against Kentucky in the East Regional Final on March 28. Few people who saw the game have ever forgotten it.

The excitement really began in the second half after Kentucky called a timeout with 11:08 left to play. The Wildcats of Kentucky were behind, 67–55, and their head coach told them, "We have Duke right where we want them. Now we make our comeback."

Over by Duke's bench, Coach K had noticed that his team thought the game was in the bag. They were easing up, and he warned them to be ready for a blitz by Kentucky.

The blitz began with Kentucky scoring 8 straight points during the next minute! The score was now 67–63 with Duke just barely leading. The crowd was buzzing. Something was brewing.

In the final 31.5 seconds, each team scored five times and the lead changed with each score. Then, with the score tied at 93, Bobby missed a jumper and the game went into overtime.

The Wildcats began the extra period by sinking a 3-pointer to lead, 96–93. Bobby tried one, but missed. The rebound was grabbed by Grant, who smartly passed back to Bobby. This time, the shot was good. Tie game.

The lead seesawed as the clock ticked down. With only 7.8 seconds left and Duke up, 102–101, Wildcat guard Sean Woods head-faked Bobby and flipped up a shot over the arm of Christian. The ball ticked off the backboard and went in. Kentucky led, 103–102, with only 2.1 seconds left on the clock.

Duke called timeout, but the situation seemed hopeless. Grant's mom started to console Antonio Lang's father, but Mr. Hill told them to sit tight.

On the floor, Coach K was telling Grant and Christian to run a special pass play that had failed against Wake Forest earlier that season. Christian would race to the foul line. If Grant could make a perfect pass and Christian could make the shot, Duke could win it.

Before play resumed, Grant could see that no one was covering him. The Wildcats had put two defenders on Christian instead. With a clear view of the whole court, Grant could see that the area by the foul line was open.

The whistle blew and Grant heaved the ball. As he watched the flight of his pass, he was reminded of scenes in the sports movies *The Natural* and *Hoosiers* in which the winning plays were shown in slow motion.

When Christian caught the pass and scored, Kentucky guard Sean Woods fell facedown on the floor. Coach K threw down his clipboard. Duke had won, 104–103. The Blue Devils were on their way to the Final Four for the fifth year in a row.

"Fate was on our side," Grant said after the game.

CHRISTIAN LAETTNER

Center/forward Christian Laettner led the Blue Devils to a 123–26 record and two national championships between 1988 and 1992. He is the first player ever to start in four Final Fours. He set NCAA tournament records for field goals attempted (167) and made (142), and by making all 12 of his free throws in the 1991 national championship game. As a senior, Christian was the National College Player of the Year and played on the U.S. "Dream Team" that won the gold medal at the 1992 Summer Olympics. He went on to play for the NBA's Minnesota Timberwolves and Atlanta Hawks. He joined Grant on the Detroit Pistons in 1999.

"We were destined. Even if somebody had been on me, even if the pass had been off, Christian would have tipped it and it would have gone in. We still would have won somehow."

Coach K didn't quite see it that way. "After the game, people talked about luck and destiny," he says. "I don't know what those things are. I just know that the ball got put in play by our best athlete. Our best player caught it and shot it."

The win over Kentucky left the Blue Devils exhausted. They struggled to beat Indiana, 81–78, a week later. Then came the championship game against the hungry and confident Michigan Wolverines on April 6.

The game was played in the Metrodome in Minneapolis, Minnesota. A crowd of 50,379 was on hand and one of the largest TV audiences in history was tuned in.

GRANT'S 1991-92 SEASON

* Led the Blue Devils with 48 dunks.
* Scored 10 or more points in 26 consecutive games.
* Took over for Bobby Hurley at point guard for five games. Led Duke to a 4–1 record while averaging 16.4 points, 6.2 rebounds, and 5.6 assists per game.
* Threw an amazing 75-foot pass to Christian Laettner, whose shot beat Kentucky in the final two seconds of the NCAA East Regional Finals.
* Had a "double-double" (18 points, 10 rebounds) against Michigan in the NCAA Championship Game.

The Blue Devils played sluggishly and fell behind, 31–30, by the end of the first half. During the halftime intermission, Coach K was so upset at his team's flat effort that he broke a blackboard in the locker room to wake them up. "When I looked at them, I wondered what was going to happen," he says.

What happened was this: Duke took off on a 23–6 run that blew the game open. Grant was on fire. In one stretch, he had 6 points, a steal, a blocked shot, and 3 rebounds. The final score was 71–51. The Blue Devils were champions again!

Bobby was named the Final Four MVP. Coach K, however, said the key to the game had been Grant, who finished with 18 points, 10 rebounds, and 5 assists.

"Grant Hill caused problems for everybody," Michigan head coach Steve Fisher said after the game. "He's quick, he's athletic, and intelligent, and those qualities make him almost impossible to stop."

Grant was asked if he thought he had a chance to win another championship and maybe even a fourth title during his senior year.

"That would be something," he replied. "We'll wait and see. Who would have thought that we would win two my first two years of college? It sounds farfetched, but it just might happen. With a little luck . . ."

Broken Dreams

I t's a fact of life in sports that the best college players are often tempted to join the NBA before they graduate. Grant was no different. He had the talent to play pro basketball, and for a time before his junior year, he considered leaving Duke. But after talking to his dad and thinking carefully, he decided not to.

"I'll definitely be at Duke all four years," he told *USA Today*. "It was stressed early on by my parents that if I didn't do well in school, I couldn't play. That has stuck with me through high school and college. My goal when I came to Duke was to graduate."

Grant's junior year promised to be an important one. Christian Laettner had graduated and moved on to the NBA. That left Bobby Hurley and Grant as the leaders of the Blue Devils.

Grant was still trying his best to stay out of the spotlight, however. He even gave his two NCAA championship rings to his dad because he didn't want to wear them and make his friends on other teams feel jealous.

Coach K wondered if Grant was ready to accept the challenge of being a leader. "A kid like Grant needs to be helped to get to his rightful position, to realize that he's really that good," he said. "Grant being Grant, he wants to be asked to advance in the line. He'll always be very sensitive toward everyone else in line, even when he's at the head of it."

Without Christian and Brian Davis, who had also graduated, Duke was no longer favored to win the national title. But once again, the Blue Devils got off to a flying start. They won their first 10 games and were ranked Number 1 in the country for five weeks.

The good start had Grant feeling confident and even a bit cocky. "Gonna score 30 on Sunday. Career high," he told a reporter from *Sports Illustrated* before a game against Georgia Tech on January 10. He was almost right — he scored 29! He also made a spectacular reverse dunk and sank 13 free throws in a row. But he missed the 14th free throw, and Duke lost by one point, 80–79. It was the Blue Devil's first loss of the season and, judging by the tough way Georgia Tech played, it was clear that other teams were gunning for the champions.

After two more wins, the Blue Devils lost to Virginia at home. The loss ended the Blue Devils' streak of 36 straight wins on their home court.

Fortunately, the Blue Devils had four days to catch

their breath before their next game. The break helped. They won seven of their next eight. Then disaster struck against Wake Forest on February 13.

There were 11 minutes to go in the first half when Grant started limping. He had hurt his left big toe. He continued to play and even started the second half, but his toe hurt so much he had to leave the game with 16:36 left to play.

Without Grant, the Blue Devils collapsed. Wake Forest's flashy forward, Rodney Rogers, burned them for 35 points, and the underdog Demon Deacons pulled off a 98–86 upset.

"Our effort just wasn't there," a disgusted Bobby said after the game. "The play that showed our attitude was when Rodney got a defensive rebound and drove the length of the court without anyone cutting him off. There's no excuse for anything like that happening."

BOBBY HURLEY

Guard Bobby Hurley was a three-time college All-America who set the NCAA records for career assists (1,076) and assists in NCAA tournament play (145). In 1993, he became Duke's all-time career leader in 3-point field goals (264). Bobby played in three Final Fours and on two national championship teams at Duke between 1989 and 1993. He was drafted by the Sacramento Kings, but suffered serious injuries in a car accident during his rookie NBA season. He recovered and joined his team in time for the next season.

The really bad news was that Grant's injury was worse than expected. It was a fractured bone. He ended up missing a month.

With Grant out, Coach K tried to help his players keep a positive attitude. "If you have the 'woe-is-me' approach, you're going to get woe is me," he told reporters. "If you take a kid's injury and say, Well, now I have an excuse for not being as good, that's woe-is-me. We just tell our team, 'Okay, here's the truth. Grant's out, probably for a couple of weeks. We don't have anybody who can do what Grant does. Now, are we going to use this to better our team?'"

Duke lost to Virginia, 58–55, in its first game without Grant, but began a decent run with four easy wins in a row. Then the Blue Devils started to struggle. They lost their final regular-season game to North Carolina, 83–69, and finished with a 24–8 record. They were ranked the Number 10 team in the country.

Having Grant back in the lineup against Georgia Tech for the first game of the ACC Tournament, on March 12, didn't help, either. Grant scored 14 points, but Duke still lost, 69–66. The Blue Devils weren't sharp, and the NCAA tournament would be starting within a week. Bobby was so concerned that he met with each one of his teammates and asked about his attitude.

His talk worked. Duke easily won its first game of

the Midwest Regionals. Then the Blue Devils faced the University of California Golden Bears. Some people thought Cal didn't have a prayer against Duke, but the Golden Bears were hot. They had won nine of their last 10 regular-season games. Plus, they had a talented point guard named Jason Kidd. Jason went on to star with the NBA's Dallas Mavericks.

The game was billed as a matchup between Jason and Bobby, who had become the NCAA's all-time career assist leader that season. As the game unfolded, Jason just kept driving into the lane and tossing passes back out to teammates, who calmly sank 3-point shots. By the end of the half, Cal was leading, 47–37.

Bobby did his all-out best to rescue the Blue Devils. He scored 32 points with 9 assists. He turned over the ball only once. Grant chipped in with 18 points, 7 rebounds, and 4 assists, but it simply wasn't enough. California won, 82–77. Duke's dream of reaching the

GRANT'S 1992–93 SEASON
* Led the Blue Devils in scoring with an 18 points per game average.
* Won the Henry Iba Corinthian Award as the top defensive player in college basketball.
* Was one of eight college players chosen to play and practice against the 1992 U.S. Olympic "Dream Team," which featured such NBA stars as Michael Jordan, Patrick Ewing, Charles Barkley, and Karl Malone.

Final Four and winning another national title was over.

Coach K was in tears after the game and he told reporters how proud he was of his players, especially Bobby and Thomas Hill, who were graduating after the season. "Losing a game doesn't mean a thing," Coach K said. "I've won so many games with these guys and I'll continue to win just for having known them."

Grant was disappointed by the loss, but he'd had a strong season. He had become one of the best players in the country. Grant had led the Blue Devils in scoring (18 points per game) and steals (64), and finished second in rebounds (6.4 per game) and blocks (36). The sweet icing on the otherwise bitter season came when he was chosen as the winner of the Henry Iba Corinthian Award as the best defensive player in college basketball.

The thought of the NBA crossed Grant's mind, but he wanted to stay. He noted, "I want to win one more national championship than Christian."

To accomplish that goal, Grant would have to accept some big, new responsibilities. "Grant has made the biggest jump with his shot and his assertiveness and being consistently excellent," Coach K said after the season. "To make the next jump, he'll need to play without Bobby and be the leader.

Being a leader was something Grant had always avoided. The big question was: Could he do it now?

Taking Charge

The 1993–94 Blue Devils were a big question mark. No one had been chosen to replace Bobby at point guard and there was a bunch of untested young players on the team. More than ever, Duke needed Grant to take charge.

Grant told reporter Mark Maske of *The Washington Post*, "I'm looking forward to leading the team. I think I'm ready for that role. I don't want to look back at this year and regret that I didn't do this or that."

In addition to leading the team, Grant was expected to do a lot more things on the court. "Grant can play every position," Coach K said before the season. "And has. And will."

Duke opened the season as the fourth-ranked team in the country. Coach K tried four different starting lineups in their first four games. He was trying to find the right combination of players, but *all* of them seemed to work. The Blue Devils won all four games!

Before the season, Grant had predicted that the team

would be good enough to reach the Final Four. Coach K wasn't so sure, but by mid-December, he was beginning to think Grant was right. In a game against the tough Michigan Wolverines, Coach K saw Grant rally his team by scoring 18 points in the final five minutes, and making all three of his 3-point shots.

By January 11th, Duke was the Number 1 team in the country. After losing a 69–68 squeaker to Wake Forest, the Blue Devils bounced back to win 12 of their next 14 games. One of the most promising signs was that guards Chris Collins and Jeff Capel were playing well. The whole team was coming together around Grant.

On February 27, Duke honored Grant by retiring his jersey number in a ceremony before the Blue Devils played Temple at home. The sellout crowd cheered as his number 33 was hung in the arena's rafters along with Bobby Hurley's 11, Christian Laettner's 32, and the numbers of earlier Duke players.

The Blue Devils went on to capture the ACC regular-season title with a record of 22–4. Then it was time to get ready for postseason play.

The ACC tournament began on March 11. Grant lit up the scoreboard with 23 points against Clemson. He was so good that night that he may have made the other Blue Devils grow lazy and feel they weren't needed as much. The next night they were dusted by Virginia, 66–61. It seemed as if Grant were playing the Cavaliers all by himself. He scored 17 points and grabbed 13 rebounds, but he tired as the game went along. In the second half, he sank only two of his 12 shots.

After the game, Coach K told the other players, "Come on, Grant can't do it alone."

Jeff Capel agreed. "We can't just sit and wait for Grant to bail us out," he told reporters after the game. "We've ridden his back all year. But he gets tired just like everyone else. We just put too much pressure on him, and that's not fair to him."

Like a true leader, Grant refused to blame the loss on his teammates or on his being tired. "I don't like to make excuses," he said. "I admit I was fatigued, but I've been fatigued before."

The 1994 NCAA tournament was only six days away, and the Blue Devils knew they had to get their act together. They had lost two of their last three games. "We just have to realize that we all need to step up," Chris Collins said.

Grant told reporters, "Coach K called me in and told me I had to be sure that I didn't accept losing. He said he knew it would be easy for me to say I've had a great career and I'm going to be playing in the NBA next year. There are no excuses left at this time of year."

Just as Bobby Hurley had done the year before,

Grant went to each of his teammates and told them, "We need everybody now. Everybody has to play."

In the NCAA tournament, Duke was placed in the Southeast Region. The Blue Devils won their first game handily. Best of all, it was a solid *team* effort.

Duke's next opponent was the Michigan State Spartans. Several top teams in the tournament, including the University of Kentucky and defending national champion University of North Carolina, had already lost in the tournament, so the Spartans were confident they, too, could pull off an upset.

"We're not the least bit afraid of Duke," said Judd Heathcote, the Spartans' head coach. "We aren't about to be intimidated by anybody."

The Spartans may not have been intimidated, but there was nothing they could do to handle Grant. He held their top scorer, guard Shawn Respert, to only one shot in the first half. Shawn came into the game with a 24.4-points-per-game average, but he didn't score a point until four minutes into the second half! Grant scored 25 points and had 7 assists, 5 rebounds, and 4 steals as Duke won comfortably, 85–74.

"Give Duke credit and give Grant credit," Shawn said after the game. "Every time I made a move, Grant was there. Nothing came easy."

The Blue Devils followed their victory over the Spartans by knocking off Marquette, 59–49, four days later. Grant was brimming with confidence. During a timeout in the second half, he told his teammates to get him the ball as much as possible because he thought he was going to get hot. Then he poured in 16 of his 22 points to lead Duke to victory.

Next came a big matchup against the Purdue Boilermakers, who were led by 6' 8" junior forward Glenn "Big Dog" Robinson. Big Dog was the leading scorer in college basketball that season. In his previous game, against Kansas, he had nailed 44 points.

The game was played in front of a sold-out crowd of 23,370 fans in Knoxville, Tennessee, on March 26. The Boilermakers raced out to a 27–17 lead with 7:35 left in the first half. Then Duke roared back with an 11–0 run over the next three minutes to lead, 28–27. But by halftime, the score was tied at 32.

Early in the second half, Grant was whistled for his fourth foul. One more and he would be out of the game, so he headed to the bench for a few minutes. During a timeout, he called his teammates around him. He told them they would have to play harder to make up for his absence.

"We knew it was time for us to step up," Jeff Capel told reporters after the game. "He had carried us. It was time to carry him. He got up to play against [Glen] and that got the rest of us ready."

The Blue Devils took the court and went to work.

When Grant returned six minutes later, Duke was up 56–50. Meanwhile, Jeff had taken over on offense and scored 15 of his 19 points in the game.

Duke went on to win, 69–60, and reached the Final Four for the third time in four years. Grant had held Big Dog to only 13 points, his lowest total of the season.

"I think I had an okay game," Grant told reporters after the game. "It was a great performance by the team. I couldn't be prouder of them. They stepped up and played like a poised team when I went out."

Just then, Big Dog Robinson walked into Duke's locker room.

"Hey, Dog," Grant said, standing up.

"Win it all, boy," Big Dog said as the two players hugged.

Grant was still hot when the Blue Devils took on the Florida Gators in the Final Four semi-finals. He ran the offense, led all scorers with 25 points, grabbed 6 rebounds, and had 5 assists. He played all 40 minutes and brought the Blue Devils back after they fell behind, 39-32, at halftime. Duke won, 70–65.

Duke's opponent in the NCAA championship game was the Arkansas Razorbacks. They were a big, quick, and very talented team that was favored to win. People wondered if Grant and his teammates had enough left to rise to the challenge.

"I won't be tired," Grant promised. "I won't allow

myself to be tired. This opportunity is one of a kind."

A reporter asked Grant if he was serious when he had said before the season that he wanted to win one more championship ring than Christian had.

"I did say that and I wasn't really joking," Grant replied. "When we go to the beach this summer, I want bragging rights. I said I thought we could win the national championship and now we've positioned ourselves to do that. I did say we'd be here and we are, so I feel good about that."

The 1994 NCAA championship game was played on April 4 at Charlotte Coliseum. A crowd of 23,674 watched the Blue Devils bravely battle the Razorbacks.

In the second half, Duke had a 13–0 scoring run. It put the Blue Devils up, 48–38, with about 17 minutes to play. The Razorbacks called timeout and regrouped. Then, during the next 8:53, Arkansas outscored Duke, 21–6, and took a 5 point lead.

With about five minutes left to play, Razorback forward Scotty Thurman noticed Grant hunched over. Grant was obviously tired and Scotty sensed that the Blue Devils were on the ropes.

Grant wasn't done yet, though. With Arkansas leading, 70–67, he sank a 3-point shot to tie the score. The Razorbacks called timeout with only 1:15 left.

When play resumed, the Razorbacks went for the

kill. Scotty Thurman took a pass on the right side of the court and found himself in a crowd of defenders. Only two seconds remained on the shot clock when he launched a rainbow. Duke's Antonio Lang jumped and just missed blocking the ball, but it went into the basket, good for 3 points. Arkansas led, 73–70, with only 52.5 seconds left to play.

Unfortunately for the Blue Devils, there would be no miracle comeback like the one against Kentucky in 1992. Arkansas held them off and won, 76–72.

The loss was disappointing for Grant, but it was no disgrace. He had played bravely, grabbing a career-high 14 rebounds to go along with his 12 points and 6 assists. As he left the court after his final game for the Blue Devils, his mother looked on with tears of pride.

All in all, it had been Grant's best season ever. He led the team in scoring (17.4 points per game). He sank 39 three-pointers. Grant had made only five threes during his first three seasons! He also led in assists, with 76, and steals, with 64. Grant's great performance

GRANT'S 1993–94 SEASON
* Was team leader in scoring (17.4 points per game), assists (5.1), and steals (1.8).
* Led the Blue Devils to their third Final Four appearance in four years.
* Won All-America and ACC Player of the Year honors.
* Had his number, 33, retired by Duke University.

earned him All-America and ACC Player of the Year honors.

Most important, Grant became a leader that season. He learned to make everyone feel like a valuable member of the team.

In May 1994, Grant graduated from Duke with a degree in history and a special place in college basketball history: He was the first ACC player ever to have more than 1,900 points, 700 rebounds, 400 assists, 200 steals, and 100 blocked shots in his career. He was truly an all-around player.

"College is the best time of your life," Grant told reporters. "It has all happened so fast. It seems like just yesterday that I was calling [assistant coach] Tommy Amaker seeking reassurance. 'Am I good enough to play at Duke?' I asked him. 'Don't worry about it,' he said."

Grant had kind words for Coach K. "Playing for Coach K for four years has been everything I could have imagined it to be," he said. "Off the court, I've learned a lot of lessons in life that will stick with me for the rest of my life. Playing for him and trying to study him has really improved my knowledge."

Coach K returned the compliment. "Grant Hill is the best player I ever coached, period," he said. "He does everything at the highest level."

Pretty soon, Grant would be doing everything at the highest level of pro basketball: the NBA.

A Young Star Among Stars

The Detroit Pistons had the third pick in the 1994 NBA Draft. The Milwaukee Bucks had the first and the Dallas Mavericks were picking second. Most people assumed the Bucks would take Big Dog Robinson and that the Mavericks wanted Jason Kidd. But rumors had been flying that the Mavericks were interested in Grant.

NBA teams were extremely impressed by the way Grant had led Duke to the 1994 NCAA championship game. They loved his intelligence, athleticism, and newfound willingness to lead his teammates. Scouts had been comparing him to Magic Johnson, Scottie Pippen, and even Michael Jordan.

The Pistons thought Grant was just the player to rescue them from their losing ways. Detroit had won NBA championships in 1989 and 1990. But when star players Isiah Thomas and Bill Laimbeer retired, and Dennis Rodman left for the San Antonio Spurs, the team collapsed. During the 1993–94 season, Detroit set a team record by losing 62 games and winning only 20.

The Pistons had no choice but to sweat and stew while Grant made some big decisions. Whom would he choose to represent him as his agent? More than 50 agents sent Grant letters. (Eventually, Grant chose Lon Babby, a lawyer from Washington, D.C.) Companies asked Grant to endorse their products. Strangers called or showed up at his door with offers.

"I'm trying to keep my head on straight," Grant told reporters. "I've tried to surround myself with people who know what's going on. They've been a great help."

Grant asked for advice from his parents, Coach K, and even Michael Jordan. "I talked with Michael during my senior year," Grant says. "I know a lot of his friends in North Carolina."

Grant visited Detroit with his dad a few weeks before the draft. He met with Pistons owner Bill Davidson, general manager Billy McKinney, and Coach Chaney. The meeting was encouraging. Grant seemed interested in playing for the Pistons.

While he was in Detroit, Grant had dinner with Joe Dumars, the team's leader. "I left the dinner very impressed with the way he presented himself," Joe says. "He was very respectful and polite."

Grant sent another hopeful signal when he told reporters, "This is definitely the best place for me. I sure hope this is where I end up. I'm all about winning and this organization is all about winning. It looks to get back to that winning tradition. I want to be a part of it."

Finally, the big day arrived on June 29, 1994. Coach Chaney had already been a nervous wreck and was now more anxious than ever. "I tried preparing myself for the letdown of not getting Grant, but I couldn't do it," he said.

The Milwaukee Bucks picked first and chose Big Dog Robinson. Then it was the Dallas Mavericks' turn. Coach Chaney held his breath. Dallas chose Jason Kidd.

"This warming rush of total relaxation ran completely through me," Coach Chaney says. "I thought to myself, 'Finally, something went right for this team.'"

Grant was delighted. He got a call of congratulations from President Bill Clinton. It was more of a gesture from a family friend than an official call from the President. (Janet Hill and Hillary Rodham Clinton had remained in touch since their college days.) Then Grant told reporters, "To me, Detroit represents everything good in professional sports. They've got players I like. They're looking to get back on top. Hopefully, we'll get there."

The Pistons gave Grant a contract that would pay him $45 million dollars to play for them for eight years. On June 30, he was introduced to the media in Detroit.

He held up a white, red, and blue jersey with number 33 on it and said, "The Pistons are getting a guy who understands that the most important thing is winning."

Grant was asked if he felt any pressure because the Pistons expected so much from him. "I don't feel any pressure," he said. "I'm just going to do what I've done all my life — play basketball and win."

Training camp opened on October 7 and Grant admits he was a bit scared at first. "I was a little nervous, anxious, excited," he says. "I didn't know what to expect. I just wanted to do a good job and try to gain respect from the other guys."

The other guys gave Grant the rookie treatment. He was called "Rook" and ordered to get coffee or anything else the veteran players wanted. "I don't mind," Grant told a reporter from *Sports Illustrated For Kids*. "Everyone has to pay their dues. The good thing is next year I'll get to mess with a rookie."

Grant spent a lot of time talking with teammates Johnny Dawkins, Bill Curley, and Rafael Addison. He became close with Joe Dumars, the last remaining member of the Pistons' championship teams, and received lots of good advice about what to expect in the coming season.

The Pistons were hoping to improve and Coach Chaney was optimistic. "I like this team," he said before the season began. "I like the way they get along and the way they compete. They can't wait to get to practice and most of them hang around afterwards. This will be a real good team in three or four years."

The Pistons opened their 1994–95 season at home against the Los Angeles Lakers on November 4th. A crowd of 21,454 was on hand in the Palace in Auburn Hills to see Grant's NBA debut. He rewarded them by leading the Pistons with 25 points and 5 assists. He added 10 rebounds and 3 blocked shots for good measure. Despite Grant's great play, Los Angeles won, 115–98.

The Pistons got off to a respectable 7–6 start. Grant averaged 19.5 points, 5.1 rebounds, and 4.5 assists in those 13 games and was named the NBA Rookie of the Month for November.

JOE DUMARS

Guard Joe Dumars is a six-time NBA All-Star and the captain of the Detroit Pistons. During his first 13 seasons in the league, he has averaged 16.4 points and 4.5 assists per game. He was named MVP of the 1989 NBA Finals in which the Pistons won the first of two consecutive championships. Joe grew up in Natchitoches, Louisiana, and went to college at McNeese State in Louisiana. The Pistons made him the 18th player chosen in the 1985 NBA Draft. In 1994, Joe was named captain of the U.S. "Dream Team II" that won a gold medal at the world championships in Toronto, Ontario, Canada.

Grant thought he could still do better. "Anytime you get an award, it's nice," he said. "But I'm into playing ball, not awards. There are a lot of things I still need to work on."

One thing Grant needed to improve was his jump shot. He had been scoring most of his points on dunks and inside shots. He worked on his jumpers every day before and after practice. "It's something I need to do," he said. "I feel confident in taking jump shots even though they don't always go in."

The hard work paid off. By December 5, Grant had become the NBA's top-scoring rookie with a 20.1 points per game average. "He has unbelievable poise for a rookie," Coach Chaney said.

Grant's rookie poise was going to be put to the test during the rest of the season. Grant was getting to be a big star in the NBA — but nobody knew just how big.

In the middle of his rookie season, Grant still found himself getting used to life in Detroit. He spent a lot of time alone and found himself missing Duke.

"In college you have your friends and there's always a lot going on," he says. "When we would go on road trips, we would check into hotels, find a piano, and play or teach each other songs. Now everybody just wants to go to sleep."

Going *anyplace* became difficult for Grant. He had become so popular that fans wanted to talk to him or get his autograph whenever they saw him. Grant tried his best to be polite, but it wasn't always easy.

"I'm just like anybody," he says. "Sometimes I'm not in the best mood. That's when you *have* to be because people take things the wrong way."

Grant loves to play video games, but going to arcades became so difficult that he ended up buying several arcade games and putting them in the basement of the three-bedroom house he rented in the town of West Bloomfield.

In less than half a season, Grant had become the most popular player in Piston history. Each week he got thousands of fan letters and several hundred requests for interviews, endorsements, and appearances. He also became the first rookie *ever* to finish first in the annual fan voting for the All-Star game!

Matt Dobek, the Pistons' vice president of public relations said, "This kid stands for all the good things about the NBA. Fans have really attached themselves to him because he's a good person."

Fans kept voting for Grant even when he couldn't play. On January 5, Grant hurt his left heel in a game against the Sacramento Kings and missed three weeks.

For the Pistons, Grant's injury was just one more setback in a season that was going sour. Nine players, including Grant and Joe Dumars, had missed time because of injury. After their good start, the Pistons were 2–11 during December. By the end of January, they were 14–26 and in last place in the Central Division.

The long, hard, 82-game season began to wear Grant down. He was used to playing only about 30 games a season in college. The competition in the NBA was also much tougher. "I'm pretty tired, really," Grant admitted after a loss in early February.

Grant's statistics for the first half of the season were quite respectable (18.4 points per game, 5.1 rebounds, 4.3 assists, and 1.8 steals). And on February 12, he got to show his stuff in the NBA All-Star Game in Phoenix, Arizona. He was a starter on the Eastern Conference team, along with Shaquille O'Neal, Scottie Pippen, Reggie Miller, and Anfernee Hardaway.

"It's just amazing," Grant told reporters his first day in Phoenix. "I am here with all these great players. I know that when I get back to my room and call my friends up, I'm going to say, 'I was in a room with Patrick Ewing,' or 'I was in a room with David Robinson.' There is still a part of me that's in awe."

The day before the game, Grant entertained kids by performing piano duets with pianist Sergio Salvatore at the NBA All-Star Stay in School Celebration. "I don't claim to be some great pianist," Grant says. "I don't even own a piano. I just play songs I like."

The next day, Grant played 20 minutes in the All-Star Game. He scored 10 points and had 3 assists and 2 steals. He made two nice dunks, but also missed four free-throws in a row.

"I was nervous, no question," he said after the game. "I was sick to my stomach. I think I did a pretty good job of hiding it. I just didn't want to go out and trip when they introduced me."

An event on March 18 finally took the attention off Grant: Michael Jordan returned to the Chicago Bulls after almost two seasons of retirement. His comeback was big, big news, and Grant was relieved that he was no longer the center of attention in the NBA.

Grant got his first chance to play against the league's most famous player on April 12 at The Palace in Auburn Hills. Michael, an excellent defensive player, covered Grant the entire game. It was quite a matchup. Grant did very well against the master, scoring 18 points with 10 rebounds and 7 assists. Michael had 29 points, 9 rebounds, and 9 assists as the Bulls won, 124–113.

Michael was impressed by Grant's performance. "It was quite an experience to watch him, although I tried not to do it too often," he told reporters after the game. "I did talk to him a little, and I told him that he was rushing a few of his shots."

The loss to the Bulls left the Pistons with only a slim hope of making the playoffs. They weren't able to do it. They finished the season with a 28–54 record, and were last in their division.

A few days after the end of the season, Pistons

general manager, Bill McKinney, resigned and head coach Don Chaney was fired. Doug Collins was named coach and general manager. He had coached Michael Jordan and the Chicago Bulls from 1986 to 1989. Coach Collins was no stranger to Grant. He is a friend of Grant's dad, and his son, Chris, was Grant's teammate at Duke. The Pistons hoped that Coach Collins could turn the team around the way he did the Bulls. Chicago had a 30–52 record the year before Coach Collins took over and then reached the playoffs the next three seasons.

Michael Jordan saw a silver lining for Grant in Detroit's cloud of failure during the 1994–95 season.

"I know what this is like for Grant, because it's hard to win all the time in college and lose like this in the pros," Michael said. "But it is also a great opportunity for him, because he can learn and make mistakes without the pressure of trying to win a lot."

Grant finished his first NBA season with a 19.9

GRANT'S 1994–95 SEASON
* Was the third player chosen in the 1994 NBA Draft.
* Became the first rookie ever to finish first in fan voting for the NBA All-Star Game.
* Led the Pistons in scoring and steals.
* Named NBA Rookie of the Year in a tie with Jason Kidd of the Dallas Mavericks — the first tie in 24 years.

points per game average. That ranked him 20th in the NBA. He averaged 6.4 rebounds and 5 assists per game. The stats stacked up pretty well with the rookie stats of one M. Jordan, who averaged 28.2 points, 6.5 rebounds, and 5.9 assists per game in 1984–85.

After the season, it was announced that Grant tied with Jason Kidd of the Dallas Mavericks for the NBA Rookie of the Year award. It was the first tie in 24 years! When Jason was in college, he played for the University of California. He was on the team that eliminated Duke from the NCAA tournament in 1993.

Grant was also named the Rookie of the Year for basketball by *The Sporting News*. This is the same award that his father had won for football 26 years before!

During the summer, Grant was among the first 10 players selected to Dream Team III. He would be part of the team that would represent the U.S. at the 1996 Summer Olympics in Atlanta, Georgia.

Grant was thrilled to be selected. "To now get the opportunity to wear red, white, and blue and represent the U.S.A. in the Olympics, well, it's the highlight of my basketball career," he said.

He meant his basketball career *so far*.

Turning Things Around

As a rookie, Grant had enjoyed a very successful season, but his team had not. When Coach Collins took the job with the Pistons, he made it clear he wanted Grant to be the player to lead his team. "Don't let that [baby] face fool you," Coach Collins said later on about Grant. "He's a tremendous competitor. I don't think a coach can ask for a better situation than to have somebody with that type of character to be your leader."

As Grant started his second season, he found himself doing more than ever. Coach Collins wanted him not only to shoot, but to direct the offense as well. That means that he starts the plays, making sure everybody is in the right place as the play begins. The reason was simple: Since Grant was Detroit's best player, Coach Collins wanted the ball in his hands as much as possible.

The Coach's plan worked. The Pistons had been one of the NBA's worst teams in the 1994-95 season. Now, just one season later, they were coming alive. Their record was steadily improving. The key was Grant.

"I guess I've kind of grown into a leadership role," Grant said. "Last year I was a rookie and didn't know how to lead or what to lead. This year we have a great bunch of guys who really work hard and are committed to winning, so it's much easier."

Off the court, fans still followed Grant's every move. He was once again the leading vote-getter for the All-Star game. In 1996, he received an amazing 1,358,004 votes! Grant scored 14 points in the game and helped the Eastern Conference team to a 129–118 victory.

At the game, Grant was introduced to one of his newest fans, baseball superstar Cal Ripken, Junior, of the Baltimore Orioles. Cal is known as baseball's "Ironman" because he played in 2,632 straight games. Cal made a point of meeting Grant and came away very impressed. He knew that Grant was a good person outside of sports, as well as a good basketball player, and he knew that the combination meant a lot.

"He seems to have a good grasp of the whole picture, how important off the court can be on the court,"

Cal said. "There's something really admirable about that."

While Grant had a blast at the February 1996 All-Star game, he was just warming up. He was hot stuff in the month of March!

The fun started on March 2 in Los Angeles against the Clippers. Grant had one of his best all-around games as a pro. He scored 35 points, which was then a career high. He also had 11 rebounds and 8 assists. More important, he sank four key free throws in the last 29 seconds to clinch a 106–101 Pistons win.

A week later, Grant was again the Pistons' star, this time against the Toronto Raptors. He scored 9 of Detroit's first 11 third-quarter points to help bring the Pistons from behind. Detroit won, 105–84. Coach Collins was amazed at all the things Grant could do.

"He guards the other teams' best perimeter shooter," Coach Collins said. "He creates shots for himself and for others. He gets to the free-throw line. He does everything."

Coach Collins wasn't the only one who noticed that Grant was performing well. Phil Jackson, who was then the Chicago Bulls coach, noticed, too. "He's doing a lot of very good things offensively. He's playing up to his potential. He's really been the key," Coach Jackson said. "Every time you look at a game in which they have a comeback or they have to get back in the ball game, it looks like he's the guy that leads the charge."

For the week of March 10 through 17, Grant was named NBA Player of the Week after leading the Pistons to a 4–0 record. In those four games, he had three triple-doubles and averaged 21.5 points, 13.3 rebounds, 8.5 assists, and 1.0 steals per game. Grant's reaction was modest as always after he was told that he had won the award. "Oh? I am?" Grant said after hearing the news. "That's my first time."

Grant's "March Madness" continued. In that month, Grant led all NBA players in rebounds with 12.8 per game. "I knew he had it in him. I didn't know how long it would take," Coach Collins said of Grant's outstanding play. "Grant is so much better now than he was at the start of the season. He has a sense that he can handle any player in the league now. He's got that kind of confidence."

Grant had another explanation for his success: a change in diet. "Last year, I lived on junk food. Last year, it was Burger King and McDonald's. It affected my play, the energy level. This year, I've been more consistent with that because I've been eating better."

Grant had hired a cook to make sure he was eating the right foods. The results paid off, even if he joked that sometimes "It seems like all I eat now is pasta." Still, Grant fought off the urge to splurge. "It kills me every day to drive by Mickey D's and see the Egg

McMuffin sign. I would stop and eat them, but I just can't have anything in my stomach before practice."

The Pistons ended the 1995-96 season with a record of 46–36. They had 18 more wins than the season before, tying a Detroit team record for the best one-season improvement. Grant became only the 15th player in NBA history to lead his team in scoring, rebounding, and assists in the same season. He averaged 20.2 points, 9.8 rebounds, and 6.9 assists a game. He led the team with an average of 1.25 steals and 40.8 minutes a game. In addition, Grant led the NBA in triple-doubles, with 10.

The improved Pistons made it into the first round of the playoffs. There they met the Orlando Magic, led at that time by Shaquille O'Neal and Penny Hardaway. The powerful Magic swept the Pistons in three straight games, but Detroit still felt it had something to celebrate. The team was better, and Grant was better. This left the players holding their heads high.

"I am disappointed we lost, but I feel good about the season," Grant said after the final game. "It wasn't pretty, but we scrapped and clawed. We put our heart and soul in everything we did."

As exciting as the season had been, Grant had more excitement ahead — the Olympics! Grant had been selected to represent his country as a member of the 1996 USA Basketball Team, called Dream Team III. Grant's teammates included such superstars as Scottie Pippen, Karl Malone, Charles Barkley, and Shaquille O'Neal. These NBA stars combined to play the best teams from other countries at the Summer Games, in Atlanta, Georgia.

Practice was perfect for Grant. "I wish the practices could be taped and people could watch them on TV," Grant said. "They were real intense. It was a lot of fun. I looked forward to practice every day."

Dream Team III dominated each game it played. Unfortunately, Grant wasn't able to play in them all. In a practice before the team's semifinal game, he injured his left knee. He couldn't play in the final two games. That included the 95–69 victory over Yugoslavia in the finals.

"It was tough to watch my teammates out there," Grant said. "You want to get out there and play. It was good to win a gold medal, but it would have been better if I had been on the court playing in the final game."

GRANT'S 1995-96 SEASON

* Led Detroit in scoring, rebounding, assists, steals and minutes played.
* Led the NBA with 10 triple-doubles.
* Was the leading vote-getter for the NBA All-Star Game receiving 1,358,004 votes.
* Was the NBA's leading rebounder for the month of March, averaging 12.8 rebounds per game.
* After the season, was a member of the U.S. Olympic basketball team that won the gold medal.

Still, "awesome" is how Grant described his Olympic experience. "Getting to spend time with athletes from around the world was great," Grant said. "An unforgettable Olympic experience for me was getting to meet [former heavyweight boxing champion] Muhammad Ali. He's a legend." Grant has called the gold medal he won his most valuable possession.

The Olympics were also another important step in Grant's becoming an NBA superstar. The more he played with his fellow Dream Teamers, the more he learned and the more confident he became. "For me, the actual playing in the games, couldn't compare to playing in practice," Grant would say. "You see how these guys prepare, see how hard they work and just getting to know them was definitely a highlight. It definitely made me a better ball player. Aside from the great memories and the feeling I had when I was on the medal stand, the one thing I took away from this experience was a lot of confidence and hopefully that confidence will show next year."

Grant realized that he truly was one of the world's best players. After holding his own against the league's superstars in U.S. Team practices, he knew he had raised his game another level. "Here are the guys I always looked up to, and now I'm playing with them," he said. "I said, 'Hey, this is the NBA's best. If I can play with Scottie Pippen every day, I can play with anybody.'"

Helping Out

The Pistons were filled with questions as the 1996-97 season began. One of them: How would they play without shooting guard Allan Houston? Allan, a free agent, had left to sign with the New York Knicks. Another problem was that the Pistons were still a very small team. Their tallest player was 6' 10." Most teams had four or five players at least that height. The Pistons would likely have trouble against bigger, stronger teams.

"I think we still have a good team here," Grant said during training camp. "We have a lot of guys who can get out and run. We can change a lot of guys around and be very productive. I think we'll make the playoffs."

Grant's words were right on target. Detroit started strong. When January rolled around, the Pistons were an amazing 22–7. Their record was second only to that of the mighty Chicago Bulls! And Grant was just getting warmed up.

Grant went on a roll in January, leading the Pistons to 10 victories in 14 games. He averaged 22 points, 9.7 rebounds, and 7.9 assists per game. For the first time in his career, he was honored as the NBA's Player of the Month. Detroit finished the regular season with a record of 54–28. It was the team's best record in seven seasons.

Grant led the team with 21.4 points, 9 rebounds, 7.3 assists, and 1.80 steals per game. He also led the NBA with an amazing 13 triple-doubles and earned a spot on the All-NBA First Team. Grant also received the IBM Award, which uses a computer formula to measure a player's overall contributions to his team's success. According to the formula, Grant was more valuable to his team than any other player in the NBA was to his team. "Being an all-around player is my game," Grant said. "It's what I do and who I am."

Teammate Joe Dumars knew that Grant deserved the honor. "Sometimes numbers are deceiving," Joe said. "His stats speak truly for what he does for this team."

GRANT'S 1996-97 SEASON

* Led Detroit in scoring, rebounding, assists, steals and minutes played, and the NBA with 13 triple-doubles.
* Named NBA Player of the Month for January.
* Voted to the All-NBA First Team and won the IBM Award for overall contributions to his team's success.

Unfortunately, Grant wasn't enough to save the Pistons in the playoffs. They faced the talented Atlanta Hawks in the first round, a best-of-five series. After splitting the first four games, the teams played the deciding game in Atlanta. Grant had 21 points, 8 rebounds and 6 assists, but they weren't enough. Atlanta's talent and size were just too much for Detroit. The Pistons lost, 84–79. Their fine season was over.

After the game, Grant once again looked at the bright side. "We made a lot of progress in two years and, hopefully, we can make a lot more in the next two years," he said. "We have to continue to move forward as a team. We all have to come back stronger and better next year."

The Pistons entered the 1997-98 season with a lot of hope. They had won 54 games the season before. Everything seemed in place for them to challenge the Bulls for the Central division crown. Instead, the Pistons sputtered. By February, they had a disappointing 21–24 record.

"This is the most frustrated I've ever been in my career," Grant told SPORTS ILLUSTRATED. "My first couple of years here, we took some steps in the right direction. But now it's like we're going backward."

With the team playing poorly, Detroit management decided to change coaches. Coach Collins was fired on February 2. The team felt that his intense, demanding style was no longer working. Assistant coach Alvin Gentry was promoted to head coach. While Grant greatly admired Coach Collins, he felt the change was a good one.

"Whatever the reason, this team was not playing the way it was capable," Grant said. "There has been a lot of speculation all season about Doug, so maybe the owner thought that was a distraction to the team. Maybe the team was so focused on that, it wasn't focused on winning."

Grant's leadership abilities were also questioned for the first time during Detroit's struggles that season. People wondered if his modest nature prevented him from being aggressive enough on the basketball court. He was known as a great guy, but was he a great player?

Grant answered his critics in a March 16 game against the Miami Heat. He got into a shoving match with 7-foot-center Alonzo Mourning of the Heat, but did not back down. Later, while racing down the court with the ball, Grant saw Alonzo under the basket. Grant decided to make a statement. He picked up the ball and jumped several feet into the air, dunking hard over Alonzo while being fouled. The play helped Detroit take control of the game and defeat Miami, 103–90.

Although the Pistons continued to struggle, Grant regained his All-Star form. On April 15, he and the Pistons shocked the world-champion Bulls, 87–79! Grant had 17 points, 9 rebounds, and 12 assists. He also did a great job of defense against Michael Jordan.

"Grant Hill was so doggone good it was unbelievable," Piston Coach Gentry said after the game. "From his passing and rebounding and points that he scored, I just thought he did as good a job as you can ever do on Michael Jordan."

Michael himself had kind words for Grant. "Grant certainly has a promising future. He can be a leader," Michael said. "It took awhile for us to do that in Chicago. Myself included. I would not give up on him."

Detroit ended its 1997-98 season with a 37-45 record, yet there were positive signs. Grant had faced tough situations on the court and he had responded, averaging an impressive 21.1 points, 7.7 rebounds, and 6.8 assists per game.

Grant felt that the difficult season made him stronger. "It's been trying at times, but I feel good about it," he told USA Today. "I'm glad I've gone through what I did. I've learned a lot. I've grown more this season than in all my years in the NBA. I feel more confident about myself and this team."

GRANT'S 1997-98 SEASON
* Led Detroit in scoring, assists, steals, and minutes played. He was second in rebounding.
* Scored 20 or more points in 44 games.
* Had four triple-doubles and 31 double-doubles.
* Was chosen to start in the NBA All-Star Game.
* Named to the All-NBA Second Team.

Working Hard for the Money

Many players use their time between seasons to relax and unwind. Not Grant. Even though he was one of the best players in the world, he still wanted to get better! That's why he hired a personal shooting coach named Chip Engellend, in the summer of 1998.

Some people might be shocked by the idea that a great player would ask for help. Grant saw things differently. "Sometimes when you're working by yourself, you're not honest," he said. "When you're by yourself, you start to justify—'Hey, I'm an all-star; I've done this and that.' But when you get an outside person, someone with a different perspective, who's going to be real honest with you, believe me, you start to look at yourself a little different."

The main thing Grant and Chip worked on was

shooting. One day, Chip made him practice one-handed shots in front of a group of 7-year-olds. "I'm shooting one-handed shots from the little dotted line near the basket, all these kids watching everything I'm doing. That was pretty embarrassing," Grant said. "And the thing about it was, when I first did it, I couldn't do it — I couldn't make the shots."

Chip was amazed at how much Grant wanted to learn. "Grant is a sponge," said Chip. "He takes in information like no player I've ever known."

The help Grant received became even more important when the 1998-1999 NBA season started late. Owners and players were trying to agree on a number of labor issues, such as how high salaries could go, and the players were locked out of practices and games by the owners. While some players hung out and took it easy until an agreement was reached, Grant kept practicing. As a result, he was really ready once the season finally began on February 8.

After winning their first two games, the Pistons took on the Washington Wizards. Grant played his best game as a pro. He started by scoring 19 points in the first quarter. By halftime, he had scored 31, on the way to a career-best 46. But that wasn't all. He also grabbed seven rebounds, dished out seven assists, plucked two steals, and blocked two shots. His last block happened on the game's final play, sealing Detroit's 106–103 win.

"Grant is a handful," Wizard head coach Bernie

Bickerstaff gushed after the game. "He's a great player."

Wizard forward Juwan Howard was also impressed. "Grant's great," he said. "He's been playing like that his whole career, since he's been in the game. I give him much respect as a player. He will continue to be great in this league, and I'm pretty sure he'll be a Hall of Famer."

Grant continued to light up the scoreboard. He won his fifth NBA Player of the Week award by leading Detroit to a 4–0 record while averaging 26.8 points, 8.5 rebounds, 5.3 assists, and 2.25 steals per game for the week ending May 2. The Pistons finished the short season with a 29–21 record.

In the playoffs, Detroit once again faced the Hawks, who had eliminated them two seasons earlier. Grant was determined not to let it happen again. However, Atlanta won the first two games and needed only one more victory to ice the series. That's when Grant and the Pistons came alive. After Detroit won Game Three, 79–63, Grant played his best playoff game ever. In only

GRANT'S 1998-99 SEASON

* Started in all 50 of Detroit's regular season games.
* Led the team in scoring, rebounding, assists, field goals, free throws made, and minutes played.
* Joined Hall of Famers Elgin Baylor and Wilt Chamberlain as the only players to lead their team in scoring, rebounding, and assists at least three times.

23 minutes, he scored 23 points to go with 9 assists, 6 rebounds, and 2 steals. The Pistons won easily, 103–82, to force Game 5.

"For two years I've been thinking about playing in a game like this," said Grant. "We've got a little momentum now, and we're feeling good."

Grant was certainly feeling good at the start of the game. He scored 10 of Detroit's first 14 points. But he couldn't keep up with another Grant: Atlanta's Grant Long, who poured in 26 points to lead the Hawks to an 87–75 victory. The season was over, but Grant's disappointment didn't last long. He had something to look forward to: getting married!

In August 1999, Grant wed his longtime girl-friend, singer Tamia Washington. The couple spent their honeymoon in Indonesia. When they returned home, Grant got back to work with Chip Engelland. He worked to improve his jump shot.

The results showed when the 1999-2000 season began. In the season opener against the Heat, Grant scored 41 points in a double-overtime loss. Even though Detroit didn't win, Grant's aggressive play set the tone for the season.

in early January, Grant had two straight 42-point games They were part of a four-game stretch in which he scored a remarkable total of 155 points. It had been 18 years since a Detroit Piston player had scored that many points in four consecutive games.

Grant's shooting percentage for the season rose to .489. He also averaged a career-high .795 free-throw percentage. As Orlando head coach Doc Rivers said, "Grant Hill has worked over the summer to make himself a better player. He's one of the Top 5 in the league and he's still working on his game. That says a lot about Grant Hill."

But the most amazing improvement was Grant's 3-point shooting. He made 34 three-pointers during the 1999-2000 season. The season before, he hadn't made any! "Right now he's probably the best total package in the league," said Magic forward Monty Williams. "Now that he has added the three-pointer to his game, he's going to be hard to stop."

Grant averaged a career-best 25.8 points per game for the season. That made him the NBA's third-leading scorer. Unfortunately, the season ended in disappointment

GRANT'S 1999-2000 SEASON
* Scored a career-high 25.8 points per game.
* Ranked third in the NBA in scoring.
* Scored 30 or more points in 29 games.
* Led the Pistons in scoring and assists.
* One of only three players to average at least 20 points, 5 rebounds, and 5 assists per game.
* Chosen to start in the 2000 NBA All-Star Game.
* Named to the All-NBA Second Team.

once more when Grant broke his left ankle. It happened in a playoff game against the Miami Heat. Grant was frustrated as the Pistons lost the series, 3–0, without him.

In Grant's six years with Detroit, the Pistons had failed to advance past the first round of the playoffs. Grant is an extremely loyal person, but he began to wonder if others in the organization wanted to work as hard to win as he did. He started to think that it might be best for him to start fresh on a new team. But which one? Plenty of teams showed interest in signing him to a contract, but he knew exactly were he wanted to go.

On August 3, 2000 the Pistons honored Grant's wish by trading him to the Orlando Magic. Along with newcomer Tracy McGrady, Grant made the Magic an instant title contender. The Magic organization wanted to win, and win now. Grant liked that attitude.

"This is the way it was at Duke," Grant said. "It feels like a winning atmosphere. That's another reason I can't wait to get started."

One of the NBA's biggest superstars had been reborn. For all the other teams, that meant one thing — trouble.

Star Power

Grant Hill's career has been a voyage of discovery. As a teenager, he had been unsure of his own basketball ability. Within a few years of turning pro, he had become a confident star in the NBA.

"It seems like yesterday I was in high school pretending I was Julius Erving, Isiah Thomas, Michael Jordan," Grant says. "Every time I stepped on the court, I was somebody else. Now I'm kind of in their shoes, in the sense that people do the same with me, so I'm told. It's just hard to believe."

During his journey to stardom, Grant discovered just how good he really is. He also learned the he had the ability to be a clutch player and a team leader.

Grant's talent, plus his humble nature, have earned him the respect of fans and opponents alike. "He's a great player, a great guy," says center Patrick Ewing of the Seattle Supersonics. "I always felt he had the ability to be the next Scottie Pippen or Michael Jordan."

Many basketball fans compared Grant to Michael and other great players when Grant entered the NBA. Grant is flattered, but knows he needs to stay true to who he really is.

"There were a lot of expectations and comparisons to Michael and Isiah [Thomas]," Grant has said of his first years in the league. "I've come to realize that I've just got to please me, my parents, my family. I can't try to be anyone else. I have to sink or swim with who I am."

Grant knows the only thing he can do is be himself. "I don't pay attention listen to comparisons. I go out and try to be Grant Hill," he said.

Getting used to being an NBA superstar has helped. "It's hard to put into words, but you just have to learn the ropes, so to speak," Grant said. "You look back at how far you've come since being a rookie and you better understand the game and the game-away-from-the-game. It's just a matter of becoming more comfortable and figuring out how to do my thing."

And Grant learned some of his most valuable lessons during his most difficult seasons. Early in 1997–98, Grant struggled with his shoot touch. His team had a disappointing record. Going through such a tough time, however, only made Grant a better player. While some players do not respond well when things go badly, Grant's never-say-die attitude helped him and his team to finish the season on a strong note.

"You're going to succeed and you're going to fail," Grant said. "It's what you do when you fail. If you bounce back, it's going to make you that much better."

One thing that makes Grant better as a person is his comfort about being a role model for children. Some pro athletes, such as former basketball star Charles Barkley, have said that athletes shouldn't have to be role models for kids. Grant does not share that opinion.

"I don't want to get [Charles] mad at me, but I have to disagree," Grant has said. "We are role models. Whether you choose to [act like] one is your decision."

When Grant was a kid, he looked up to his parents. In sports, he admired pro basketball legend Julius "Dr. J" Erving for the classy way he acted on and off the court. Grant also admired pro tennis player Arthur Ashe. In 1975, Arthur became the first African-American male to win the mens singles championship at the famous Wimbledon tournament. He earned a lot of respect by helping charities and speaking out for the African-American people before he died, in 1993.

For his part, Grant promotes reading by being a spokesman for the American Library Association. He is also very involved with the Special Olympics, which is an international program of year-round sports training and athletic competition for more than one million children and adults with mental retardation. Grant first volunteered to help with the Special Olympics when he was in high school, in Virginia. He has remained involved all the way through college and into the NBA.

"When I'm 40, I hope people talk about me the same way [that they do about Arthur]," Grant says. "When you're growing up, you try to have role models. My parents stressed the importance of education, athletics, and the right people. I didn't have to go outside my house for any of that. Everything I needed, everything I had to hear, was right at home."

Calvin Hill is very proud of Grant. He's happy that people think of him as Grant's dad, instead of as a former NFL star. "The fact that people recognize me as his father is great," he says. "If I can be defined by my son, that's okay by me. My greatest accomplishment is being a

---

GRANT'S FAVORITE THINGS

Sport to Watch (other than basketball): Football
Sport to Play (other than basketball): Soccer
Athletes: Jerry Rice and Anfernee (Penny) Hardaway
Colors: Blue and black
Food: Seafood gumbo
Book: *Days of Grace* by Arthur Ashe
Singers: Boyz II Men
Song: "Two Occasions" by The Deele
Place to Be (when not playing basketball): A video-game arcade
Video Game: *Galaga*

father. Watching your kid accomplish something is much bigger than scoring a touchdown."

Even though he's grown up and a superstar, Grant knows that he's not too old for advice from his parents. "I usually speak to one of them every day," Grant said. "They have been very supportive and instrumental in my life and my success, and they continue to be."

Another person who helped Grant is his former teammate Joe Dumars. When they were together on the Detroit Pistons, they spent a lot of time talking about basketball and life. One of the things that Joe liked about Grant is that the success of the team always comes before any individual goals. "Any player worth his salt wants to see his team do well and Grant is defintely worth his salt," Joe says.

Striving for success is what keeps Grant going. He has set very high goals for himself and the Orlando Magic, but there is no reason to think that he can't achieve them. Says his dad: "What motivates Grant is to show that his success has nothing to do with what he is given and everything to do with what he *earns*."

The one thing that Grant wants to earn is an NBA championship. He knows that great players are often judged by how many titles they win, and he feels his time is drawing near. How often does he think about it?

"Every day," Grant says. "It's my number-one goal,

my number-one priority, to win a championship. Hopefully, when all is said and done, I will have one, at least one, maybe two, as many as I can win."

Grant thinks about winning a championship so much and so intensely that he has trouble watching other teams play for the title. "It's fun, but, also, it's hard," he says of watching the NBA Finals. "Because you want to be there and see how much fun it is and how the whole world is focusing on the championship series. It makes you want to get there and makes you want to focus in on what you're doing."

But even Grant knows that championships do not happen over night. Great teams take time to build, and the Magic are still trying to fit all their new pieces into the championship puzzle.

"A basketball season, a career, even life — it's a marathon, not a sprint," Grant says. "You're going to have moments when you feel as if you can't make it. You're going to have moments when you catch your second wind. That's what this is. A marathon."

Grant knows that every basketball career has its share of highs and lows. The key for him is maintaining a steady confidence through good times and bad. When asked about the most important thing that a coach ever told him, Grant replies: "You're never as good as your best game and you're never as bad as your worst game. Regardless of how well or how badly you play, you just try and take the very same approach into every game."

That approach has helped make Grant a basketball success story. The shy, skinny high-schooler from Reston, Virginia has grown up to become an international superstar. But is there anything he would change about his career?

"I wouldn't change a thing," Grant says. "I've been fortunate to have played with some great players and for some great coaches, and to accomplish — in high school, college, and, hopefully, at this level — a lot of wonderful things. I'm lucky and grateful for that. I just want to continue to get better."

That shouldn't be a problem. Grant seems to get better every year. "I'm entering my prime," he says. "I've reached the point where I still have my athleticism and youthfulness, but I also have the

---

INSIDE GRANT

Biggest Sports Thrill: Winning my second NCAA Basketball Championship at Duke, in 1992

The Place I Would Most Like To Visit: An island in the Caribbean

The Person I Would Most Like to Meet: Michael Jackson

The Best Advice I Ever Received: "Whatever you do, try to do and be your best." — from my dad

Secret ambition: To run for political office

The Person I Admired Most When I Was a Kid: My dad

smarts, the experience, to make it work. I can do things now that I couldn't do two, three years ago."

But it all comes down to Grant's favorite two words: hard work.

"We know we've got a lot of hard work ahead of us," he says of the Magic. "But, ultimately, that's our goal . . . to win a championship."

WANT TO HAVE MORE FUN

WITH SPORTS ILLUSTRATED FOR KIDS?

GET A FREE TRIAL ISSUE of SPORTS ILLUSTRATED FOR KIDS **magazine**. Each monthly issue is jam-packed with awesome athletes, super-sized photos, cool sports facts, comics, games, and jokes!

Ask your mom or dad to call and order your free trial issue today! The phone number is 1-800-732-5080.

PLUG IN TO www.sikids.com. That's the S.I. FOR KIDS website on the Internet. You'll find great games, free fantasy leagues, sports news, trivia quizzes, answers to your questions about sports, and much, much more.

CHECK OUT S.I. FOR KIDS **Weekly** in the comic section of many newspapers. It has lots of cool photos, stories, and puzzles from the Number 1 sports magazine for kids!

LOOK FOR more S.I. FOR KIDS **books**. They make reading **fun!**